The Values of Science

The Oxford Amnesty Lectures Series

The Values of Science: Oxford Amnesty Lectures 1997,
edited by Wes Williams

Women's Voices, Women's Rights: Oxford Amnesty Lectures 1996,
edited by Alison Jeffries

The Values of Science

The Oxford Amnesty
Lectures 1997

EDITED BY
Wes Williams

Westview Press
A Member of the Perseus Books Group

Copyright © 1999 by Westview Press, A Member of the Perseus Books Group

Published in 1999 in the United States of America by Westview Press, 5500 Central Avenue, Boulder, Colorado 80301-2877, and in the United Kingdom by Westview Press, 12 Hid's Copse Road, Cumnor Hill, Oxford OX2 9JJ

Library of Congress Cataloging-in-Publication Data
The values of science : the Oxford amnesty lectures 1997 / edited by
  Wes Williams.
    p. cm.
  ISBN 0-8133-6757-3
  1. Science—Philosophy.   2. Human rights.   I. Williams, Wes.
Q175.3.V35   1998
303.48'3—dc21   98-34629
                                                                             CIP

The paper used in this publication meets the requirements of the American National Standard for Permanence of Paper for Printed Library Materials Z39.48-1984.

10   9   8   7   6   5   4   3   2   1

Contents

Preface to the Oxford Amnesty Lectures

A single idea governs the Oxford Amnesty Lectures. Speakers of international reputation are invited to lecture in Oxford on a subject related to human rights. The public is charged to hear them. In this way funds are raised for Amnesty International, and the profile of human rights is raised in the academic and wider communities.

The organisation of the lectures is the work of a group of Amnesty supporters. They act with the approval of Amnesty International, but are independent of it. Neither the themes of the annual series nor the views expressed by the speakers should be confused with the views of Amnesty itself. For each annual series a general theme is proposed, bringing a particular discipline or perspective to bear on human rights. The speakers are invited to submit an unpublished lecture, which is delivered in Oxford; the lectures are then published as a book.

Amnesty International is a worldwide human rights movement that is independent of any government, political faction, ideology, economic interest, or religious creed. The Amnesty International mandate is as follows: to seek the release of prisoners of conscience—people imprisoned solely for their beliefs, colour, ethnic origin, language, or religion, provided that they have neither used nor advocated the use of violence; to oppose the death penalty, torture, or other cruel, inhuman, or degrading treatment or punishment of all prisoners; to end extrajudicial executions or "disappearances"; and to oppose abuses by opposition groups—hostage taking, the torture and killings of prisoners, and other arbitrary killings.

The members of the Committee of the Oxford Amnesty Lectures 1997 were Madeleine Forey, John Gardner, Chris Miller, Fabienne Pagnier, Deana Rankin, Stephen Shute, and Wes Williams.

Acknowledgments

The production of a book such as this is a collaborative effort. Good committee members take turns to shoulder responsibilities; the greater share of the organisation of the lectures themselves was undertaken by Deana Rankin. This is the first of the Oxford Amnesty books in which there has been a division of labor between editor and introducer. I am grateful to Jonathan Rée for responding to the challenge of introducing so diverse a set of lectures and for doing so with such good grace. To the lecturers themselves, particular thanks are due. All contributors to the Oxford Amnesty Lectures give of their time and expertise freely. Contributors to this volume have been more than generous in response to the demands I have made on their patience and their goodwill during the preparation of the lectures for publication. It has been a privilege to work with the texts of people who write with such wit, passion, and integrity; I am most grateful to them.

W.W.

1

Introduction: Nature, Values, and the Future of Science

Jonathan Rée

As I walked into Christopher Wren's magnificent Sheldonian Theatre to listen to the first of the 1997 Oxford Amnesty Lectures on "The Values of Science," I found myself thinking about my first chemistry lesson at school. The topic was combustion, but our teacher began with a short lecture on the nature of science. Science is based purely on observation, he said, and it goes back to the seventeenth century (just like the Sheldonian) to the "scientific revolution," in which Europe shook off the superstitions of the Dark Ages and woke up to the objective reality of the world of nature as revealed to the senses.

At the end of the lesson, our teacher told us all to write a paragraph describing what happens when a piece of paper burns, and I obediently recorded a whole range of objective facts garnered from observation: the way you strike a match and apply it, for best effect, to a torn edge of the paper; the flames that lick and flicker and vary in color from rim to centre and from tip to root; the acrid smell of the smoke; and the ragged shapes of the charred scraps left behind.

The teacher was dismayed that I had so misunderstood his point about science and observation: the facts we were meant to establish were those set out in the first chapter of our textbook, not those we knew from our own experience. I took his point and became a good enough chemistry student. But a seed of doubt had been sown in my mind: do scientists really understand the nature of their craft?

The lecture in the Sheldonian that evening was by Richard Dawkins, and he struck a note of panic that came as rather a surprise to me and, I think, to most of the rest of the audience. Instead of considering possible conflicts between modern science and human rights, he painted a portrait of contemporary scientists as a beleaguered minority, victimised by hordes of "cultural relativists" merely for their belief that "there is something almost sacred about nature's truth." The "fashionable prattlings" of the relativists, he said, were endangering the very survival of "objective truth which transcends cultural variety." He proposed to put on the mantle of a "modern Rider Haggard hero" and ride to the rescue of scientists suffering persecution "for valuing simple truth." If the "savages of relativism" were allowed to succeed, Dawkins warned, we would descend into "a new Dark Age," and he for one would "not wish to go on living."

Nature and Progress

As it happened, I had just been reading Samuel Butler's *Erewhon*, a fictional description of an isolated antipodean civilisation which—like the Dark Age of Dawkins's nightmare—has freed itself from science. The narrator of this inverted utopia, first published in 1872, is a European traveller who at first takes Erewhonian society to be a freakish survival from prehistory. But then he discovers that the citizens of Erewhon had long ago reached a level of scientific development that Europe did not approach until the nineteenth century. The intellectuals of twelfth-century Erewhon foresaw a future where scientists would build machines possessing consciousness and a will of their own, whilst humanity would be reduced to "a sort of parasite upon the machines" or "an affectionate machine-tickling aphid." To avert this disaster, they fostered a counter-scientific revolution under the leadership of the "anti-machinist" party, and the social fabric of Erewhon was eventually saved through the timely elimination of science. Ever since then, Colleges of Unreason had provided the sons of rich families with a humane education in a dead language called Hypothetics, in which they could invent "utterly strange and impossible contingencies" and "give intelligent answers to the questions that arise therefrom," without ever encountering any notions of science or "progress." In the meantime, ordinary Erewhonians were left to lead full and innocent lives of inefficient manual labor, without clocks or machines to disturb the natural rhythms of their days.[1]

Is this, I wondered, the future Dawkins fears? Butler's Erewhonians might be happy and intelligent in their way, but there could be no doubt that in giving up on science they had given up on progress too. It is not just that science makes labor more productive and expands the amenities of human existence; nor is it merely that the light of science may stimulate the growth of the mind, rather as the light of the sun stimulates the growth of plants. The connection between science and progress is not merely contingent: ever since the publication of Francis Bacon's *Advancement of Learning* in 1605, the career of scientific knowledge has always been defined as an inexorable movement from occasional outcrops of anecdote to vast fields of uniform information, or from uncoordinated hypotheses and rules of thumb to huge articulated networks of theory. It is part of the definition of a science, in other words, that it should have a cumulative and progressive history, and thinking about science has always meant thinking about where it will take us next—in the coming decade, century, or millennium. It is not a coincidence that the author of *Advancement of Learning* should have written not only a *New Organon* of scientific method but also a *New Atlantis* of scientific fantasy. From Bacon to Dawkins, those who have taken it on themselves to defend science against its supposed enemies have been less interested in describing past achievements than in punting on those to come. The rhetoric of science has always been a rhetoric of futurity.

On the face of it, the taste for prophecy and soothsaying amongst the friends of science is quite paradoxical. Surely Isaac Newton and the other seventeenth-century pioneers were interested only in well-established facts, and surely they chose the word "nature" to describe their subject matter precisely in order to emphasise its eternal uniformity and its immunity from historical change? At the same time, however, they did not resist the temptation to personify nature, treating it as a kind of Sovereign Power or Supreme Being or, indeed, as grim Fate itself. The "system of the world" that forms the third and final part of Newton's *Philosophiae Naturalis Principia Mathematica* (published in 1687) opens by stating certain "rules of reasoning," which are phrased not as canons of logic but as descriptions of nature's peculiar tastes and conduct. "Nature is pleased with simplicity," says the first rule, "and affects not the pomp of superfluous causes." And, as Newton says in another: "we are certainly not to . . . recede from the analogy of nature, which is wont to be simple, and always consonant to itself."[2]

Another of nature's personality traits was its secretiveness and the pleasure it evidently takes in giving us misleading clues as to its private operations. To use Newton's examples, nature leads us to see earthly and celestial events—"the light of our culinary fire and the sun," say, or "the reflection of light in the earth, and in the planets"—as qualitatively different from each other, when in fact it governs them all with exactly the same universal mathematical principles. Despite the bewildering diversity which it presents to ordinary experience, nature is in fact a creature of extraordinarily regular and uniform habits; indeed, one only has to look at the solar system from the proper point of view to see that all its fundamental operations can be represented by a rigid clockwork model as simple as a child's toy. (History might have been different if Newton had had to reckon with a solar system comprising hundreds of different bodies, instead of just Mercury, Venus, and Mars; followed by Saturn and Jupiter, each with four attendant satellites; and then the Earth, the Moon, and the Sun: a manageable little family with only fifteen members, all of them extremely predictable in their behavior.)

It is possible to regard the impassive equability of Newtonian nature not as a step beyond the Christian idea of a benevolent divine providence but as a return to a heathen conception of loveless divinities which are indifferent to our happiness or even hostile to it; and that was certainly how it struck George Berkeley. In his *Treatise Concerning the Principles of Human Knowledge* (1710), Berkeley argued that Newton, abetted by his philosophical apostle John Locke, was giving succour to "materialists" and thus opening a path that would lead directly to "Scepticism, Atheism and Irreligion." Berkeley did not dispute Newton's mathematical descriptions of phenomena, but he objected to the presumption that they reflected "laws" which derived from something called "matter," "corporeal substance," or "nature." The word "nature," he said, was just "an empty sound, without any intelligible meaning annexed to it," or a "vain *chimera* introduced by those heathens, who had not just notions of the omnipresence and infinite perfection of God." Like bad money driving out good, the idea of "the clockwork of Nature" threatened to drive out the perfectly sound and seemly notions of spirit and will that are embedded in ordinary pious common sense.[3]

Of course, Newton had not intended his portrayal of nature as an insult to humanity or religion, and neither had Copernicus, Galileo, or Descartes. It is possible to interpret natural science and revealed religion in ways that enable them to live together without any affront to the canons of logic: after all, there is no scientific necessity to insist that material nature is the ultimate reality, and there is no theological obstacle to supposing that God contrived the world so that it would appear to us as if governed by autonomous laws of nature.

But Berkeley was right to expect that Newton's concept of nature would be used to assail both religion and human dignity. During the eighteenth century, the more vociferous of the self-proclaimed friends of science began to treat the general offensiveness of a proposition as if it were in itself a criterion of scientific validity, and they instituted a new kind of intellectual sport: mocking and humiliating those who (as it seemed to them) were too timid to let go of the "spiritualist" view that humanity occupies a special position in the natural world. They did not even entertain the possibility that scientific materialism could be criticised in good faith. The French physician Julien Offray de La Mettrie, for example, wrote exuberantly about how humans were nothing but complex animals and animals nothing but complex machines. Judgement, reason, and memory were nothing but modifications of the medullary substance in our heads, he said, and we think with our brains just as we walk with our legs. It was only fond pride that made anyone cling to the doctrine of the immateriality and indivisibility of the soul; and it was mere wishful weakness that made us want to hive off our moral or mental qualities, vainly imagined as controlled by free will, and segregate them from our bodily existence as part of the mighty machinery of the natural world. In particular, our sexual organs were as worthy of our humanity as our brains, and we should swallow our petty vanity and realise that the only route to happiness lies through atheism. "We honor man," as La Mettrie said, "by placing him amongst the animals."[4]

The jeering tones of La Mettrie's materialism were amplified in the nineteenth century, after Darwin had revealed a mechanism of "natural selection" that was as indifferent to human preferences as Newton's "powers of nature." And ever since the 1920s, Darwinian prophets like J. B. S. Haldane have delighted in shocking humane sentiment by advocating scientific selection of the characteristics of future human beings. "The biologist is the most romantic figure on earth," he wrote in *Daedalus, or Science and the Future* in 1923. The "application of biology to politics" was an urgent imperative, and if we ignored it we could be sure that "civilization would have collapsed" by the end of the twentieth century.[5]

Values and Morality

Listening to Richard Dawkins that evening, as he gave the first of the Amnesty Lectures to be published in this volume, I was reminded of La Mettrie and Haldane. Civilisation or barbarism: the only way to avoid a new Dark Age, Dawkins argued, was by trusting to science. He prophesied that future natural science would be able to explain our choices of "values" in terms of evolutionary psychology, but emphasised that it would never be able to advise us as to what values we ought to choose. Nature delights in "cutting humanity down to size," he said, and in rebuking our absurd self-importance: "Nature, fortunately, is indifferent to anything so parochial as human values."

But, as the environmental campaigner George Monbiot reminded us a few days later when he spoke about biotechnology, human values matter to human beings, if not to nature itself. Monbiot pointed out that however successful it may be as an objective description of nature's ways, biotechnology is also a force in commerce and politics. The social consequences of science are a matter of more than scientific concern, he argued, and we would be failing in our duty as citizens if we did not reserve the right to work out our moral priorities for society and impose them, if necessary, on irresponsible scientists and their managers.

Supporters of Richard Dawkins might dismiss Monbiot's concern with the politics of science as a piece of unscientific emotionalism, but Dawkins himself had concluded his lecture by urging us, in the name of science, to "invent our own values" and "sit down together and work out the values we want to follow." Even if we could imagine Dawkins and Monbiot entering into some kind of ethical peace process, however, it is hard to be optimistic about the outcome: one party was already signed up to the values of science, the other to human values, and there seemed to be no way of bridging the gap between them.

The difficulty is that there is no neutral way of conceptualising the issues that divide them. Indeed, the very word "values" already biases the discussion. It was introduced into eighteenth-century moral theory from partisan motives, by materialistic thinkers who took masochistic pleasure in the thought of nature's cool indifference to the moral distinctions that we humans like to live by. Jeremy Bentham and other radical utilitarians attempted to fashion a new moral logic, one that would follow natural science by relying on methods of quantitative calculation rather than qualitative deliberation. For them, morality was like the market: it did not dictate what people ought to want but simply responded impersonally and impartially to whatever preferences they expressed. In short, morality, like economics, was a matter of "values."

The word suggested a neat separation of powers between science and morality, based on a metaphysical dichotomy between objective scientific facts and subjective moral preferences; but by abandoning the idea that there were rational grounds for preferring one value to another, it whiteanted morality and took the moral pith out of it. Bertrand Russell was lucid about the consequent devastation, though he saw no way of averting it. If people differ about values, he wrote, then "there is not a disagreement as to any kind of truth, but a difference of taste." Values, he explained, are composed not of statements about the world but of arbitrary desires that we happen to feel "subjectively" within ourselves. Science might help us pursue the values we happen to have, but it could never tell us what values we ought to adopt. "Science has nothing to say about 'values,'" he wrote, and "what science cannot discover, mankind cannot know."[6]

But Russell's understanding of the crucial role science can play in human affairs did not prevent him from criticising it. "Science threatens to cause the destruction of our civilization," he wrote in *Icarus, or the Future of Science*, published in 1924 as a riposte to Haldane's vision of a future in which politics would be saved by biologists. Russell dismissed the idea that "the progress of science must necessarily be a boon to mankind," saying that it was "one of the comfortable nineteenth-century delusions which our more disillusioned age must discard." If science had taught us that morality is a matter of taste, then it could not object if we came to the conclusion that science itself is immoral: "Science is no substitute for virtue," as he put it. No one could deny that "science enables the holders of power to realize their purposes more fully than they could otherwise do," but since "the purposes of the holders of power are in the main evil," it followed that "science does harm."[7] If Russell was alive today, he would almost certainly have been on Monbiot's side rather than Dawkins's.

Nature, Morals, and Relativism

A few days later, Nicholas Humphrey mounted the podium and developed an argument which cut right across these familiar lines of debate. He denied the assumption that questions of morality are distinct from those of science. For him, science is itself a moral good and therefore a fundamental human right. Children everywhere, he argued, deserve to be taught "the modern scientific worldview"—not because it will make them prosperous but simply because it is the truth. Moreover, society has a positive duty to protect children from falsehood and nonsense: "We should no more allow parents to teach their children to believe, for example, in the literal truth of the Bible, or that the planets rule their lives," he said, "than we should allow parents to knock their children's teeth out or lock them in a dungeon."

Humphrey's proposal made the audience very uneasy: the idea of imposing modern science on everyone regardless of their backgrounds and preferences seemed like sheer brainwashing and scarcely compatible with the aims of Amnesty International. But I found myself wanting to defend him. He was not advocating indoctrination, after all, since—as far as he is concerned at least—science is not one doctrine amongst others; indeed, it is not a belief system at all but simply a willingness to follow "critical reasoning" wherever it may lead. That was why he considered it a duty to give everyone an education in science: science, for him, is the essence of intellectual autonomy.

Support for the idea of science as a cultural value came with John Barrow's description of how scientific interest has recently shifted from simple and universal laws of nature of the kind formulated by Newton towards the study of complexity and chaos. We may have grown accustomed to the idea of science as a search for regularities, and we may be either excited or appalled by the idea of a "Theory of Everything." But, if Barrow is right, we can relax: there will always be mysteries that science has not explained. No scientific theory will ever be final, and the culture of science is essentially open-ended.

But then I listened to Daniel Dennett, and the scope of science seemed to narrow again. Like Dawkins, he recounted close encounters with unnamed relativists, in this case "an eminent and fashionable literary theorist" who wanted to have a "new and different and stylish" theory of knowledge and did not care whether it was true, sound, or even defensible. Taking fright at this monstrosity, Dennett gave a sturdy defence of the "faith in truth," which he takes to be the distinctive creed of the scientist. He presented this faith as a distillation of a universal human ability to tell the difference between appearance and reality, which is itself rooted, he said, in the evolutionary necessity that an organism "get it right" in matters affecting its survival or that of its offspring. The concept of truth, Dennett concluded, is both universal and indispensable because evolution makes it so.

But Dennett must surely have been a little dazzled by his "fashionable literary theorist" if he thinks his evolutionary defence of truth sufficient to deflect "relativistic" criticisms of science. Relativists must by definition deny that the distinction between truth and falsehood is absolute, but that does not mean that they deny the distinction absolutely or claim that ignorance is just as good as knowledge. Being relativists merely makes them wary of the assumption, which Dennett seemed to have swallowed whole, that science must subsume all other kinds of knowledge.

Dennett's inflation of the concept of science reminded me of what had made the audience in Oxford uneasy with Nicholas Humphrey's argument for compulsory science education for all. Humphrey, like Dennett, played a wide game with a trash-all category of "nonscience": it included falsehood, dogma, and superstition but also, implicitly and by casual oversight, the understanding of languages, poetry, and philosophy—not to mention history, including the history of science and of the kinds of fantasy-futurology in which scientists like to engage. In other words, Humphrey overlooked the fact that if children have a universal right to grow up free from superstition, then they have a right to be protected from scientism too—that is to say, from the dogma that what science does not know is not knowledge.

In the wise and wide-ranging philosophical survey which concluded the whole series, Mary Midgley argued against precisely this idea of "omnicompetent science." It is one of three unfortunate "myths" of the European Enlightenment, she argued, alongside the myth of the social contract and the myth of progress. Admirable as it is in itself, she said, science becomes dangerous if we detach it from its human historical context and turn it into a fetish, even a substitute religion.

It occurred to me that Midgley could have added a fourth item to her list of myths: that of the "fashionable" relativists (or, to give them a more current name, "postmodernists") and the threat they pose to science and civilization. Midgley had the misfortune of being the only contributor to the series who bore much resemblance to the ogres that exercised Dawkins, Humphrey, and Dennett. In daring to criticise the excesses of science, had she not revealed herself to be its relativistic enemy?

But that, I now felt sure, was a false alternative. One does not have to be an enemy of science to be an admirer of forms of knowledge that are not and never will be scientific. Take combustion, for example: we all know something about it even without the benefit of a chemistry lesson; indeed, we would not be able to make much sense of chemistry unless we had this kind of prescientific knowledge to build on. Painters and poets know lots of things about fire, and so do fire-fighters, cooks, foresters, and blacksmiths; so too did natural philosophers before the seventeenth century. Their knowledge is not scientific, but that does not stop it from being well grounded and indeed objective—objective enough, at least, to have as close a bearing on the survival of the species as a whole library of far-out scientific monographs. I found I could no longer understand why the friends of science are determined to treat relativism as their enemy.

And I recalled that throughout much of its history, relativism has in fact been closely associated with natural science. Relativism is primarily a doctrine about morality or values, based on the homely observation that different societies organise their lives in different ways and that there is no universally agreed method by which one way of life could ever transcend all the others and establish its absolute moral supremacy. The main proponents of relativism have not been enemies of science but exactly the opposite: enthusiasts in the tradition of La Mettrie, who have argued that science is about nature, that nature contains material facts rather than moral values, and that morality must therefore be a matter of personal taste.

Some time in the 1960s, however, the tables were turned. Those who would now be called "postmodernists" began to note that if the fundamental variousness and nonconvergence of moral opinions (which, in any case, is often exaggerated) discredits the idea of absolute moral knowledge, then the fundamental variousness and nonconvergence of scientific opinions (which is often underestimated) must equally discredit the idea of absolute natural science. If the partisans of science are now troubled by the spectre of relativism, perhaps it is only the ghost of their attitude toward morality that has come back to haunt them.

When the lectures were all over and I was leaving the Sheldonian for the last time, I thought back to Richard Dawkins's formulation of the problem of values and science a month before. I realised that what had worried me was not only his assumption that science is the only form of knowledge but also a certain inequity in his attitudes toward morality and natural science. He had told us that "absolutist" interpretations of morality are undermined by modern evolutionary theory, which shows that the ethical distinctions that are salient for us have more to do with strategies for genetic survival than with absolute moral realities that exist in nature apart from us. But if that argument applies to morality, I thought, it must surely apply to science too, demonstrating that the scientific distinctions that work for us have more to do with our biological inheritance than with absolute natural realities. Indeed, if Dennett is right, then that is as much as we could ever really mean by calling scientific values truths.

And I noted that if the friends of science could be persuaded to be as relativistic about science as they want to be about morality, such an attitude need not compromise the dignity of scientific endeavour. On the contrary: if science is really suffering a deficit of intellectual esteem, then it might get a fillip if scientists were recognised as using their imaginations to invent new ways of objectively apprehending the world and not simply stumbling into objects that were lying around all along. All relativism can really mean, after all, is that judgements are always made in relation to some standard and that these standards depend on specific historical circumstances—on learning a particular calculus, perhaps; or how to use an experimental apparatus; or even sitting in a beautiful old building listening to the Amnesty Lectures and connecting them to memories of schooldays or to the books that happen to be on our mind at the time. The fact that knowledge always has individual roots is hardly an argument against its objectivity, and relative truth and progress are still truth and progress. In fact I was finding it increasingly difficult to imagine what other kinds there could be. If the objectivity of science needs defending, then it might be better to start by acknowledging the relativity of our knowledge rather than anxiously trying to deny it. If we could all agree on that, I thought, then future friends of science will reach an understanding with future critics, and we will end up as critical friends of science.

Notes

1. Samuel Butler, *Erewhon: Or Over the Range* (1872; reprint, London: Jonathan Cape, 1908), pp. 225, 245, 218.

2. Isaac Newton, *Mathematical Principles of Natural Philosophy* (1687), trans. Andrew Motte, rev. Florian Cajori (Berkeley: University of California Press, 1934), vol. 2, pp. 398–399.

3. George Berkeley, *Treatise Concerning the Principles of Human Knowledge, wherein the Chief Causes of Error and Difficulty in the Sciences, with the Grounds of Scepticism, Atheism and Irreligion, are inquired into* (1710), pt. 1, sects. 60, 150.

4. Julien Offray de La Mettrie, *L'homme machine* (1748; reprint, Paris: Pauvert, 1966), pp. 85, 128, 95, 119.

5. J. B. S. Haldane, *Daedalus, or Science and the Future* (London: Kegan Paul, Trench, Trubner, 1923), pp. 78, 57–67. This text was originally issued as part of the "Today and To-morrow" series, edited by C. K. Ogden.

6. Bertrand Russell, *Religion and Science* (London: Thornton, Butterworth, 1935), pp. 237–238, 223, 243.

7. Bertrand Russell, *Icarus, or the Future of Science* (London: Kegan Paul, Trench, Trubner, 1924), pp. 63, 57–58.

2

The Values of Science and the Science of Values

Richard Dawkins

The values of science, what does this mean? In a weak sense I shall mean—and shall take a sympathetic view of—the values that scientists might be expected to hold, insofar as these are influenced by their profession. There is also a strong meaning, in which scientific knowledge is used directly to derive values as if from a holy book. Values in this sense I shall strongly repudiate. The book of nature may be no worse than a traditional holy book as a source of values to live by, but that isn't saying much.

The science of values—the other half of my title—means the scientific study of where our values come from. This in itself should be value-free, an academic question, not obviously more contentious than the question of where our bones come from. The conclusion might be that our values owe nothing to our evolutionary history, but that is not the conclusion I shall reach.

The Values of Science in the Weak Sense

I doubt if scientists in private are less (or more) likely to cheat their husbands or their tax inspectors than anybody else. But in their professional lives scientists do have special reasons for valuing simple truth. The profession is founded on a belief that there is such a thing as objective truth which transcends cultural variety and that if two scientists ask the same question, they should converge upon the same truth regardless of their prior beliefs or cultural background or even, within limits, ability. This is not contradicted by the widely rehearsed philosophic belief that scientists don't prove truths but advance hypotheses which they fail to *disprove*. The philosopher may persuade us that our facts are only undisproved theories, but there are some theories we shall bet our shirt on never being disproved, and these are what we ordinarily call true. Different scientists, widely separated geographically and culturally, will tend to converge upon the same undisproved theories.

This view of the world is poles away from fashionable prattlings like the following:

> There's no such thing as objective truth. We make our own truth. There's no such thing as objective reality. We make our own reality. There are spiritual, mystical, or inner ways of knowing that are superior to our ordinary ways of knowing. If an experience seems real, it is real. If an idea feels right to you, it is right. We are incapable of acquiring knowledge of the true nature of reality. Science itself is irrational or mystical. It's just another faith or belief system or myth, with no more justification than any other. It doesn't matter whether beliefs are true or not, as long as they're meaningful to you.[1]

That way madness lies. I can best exemplify the values of one scientist by saying that if there comes a time when everybody thinks like that, I shall not wish to go on living. We shall have entered a new Dark Age, albeit not one "made more sinister and more protracted by the lights of perverted science"—because there won't be any science to pervert.[2]

Yes, Newton's Law of Gravitation is only an approximation, and maybe Einstein's General Theory will in due season be superseded. But this possibility does not lower them into the same league as mediaeval witchcraft or tribal superstition. Newton's laws are approximations that you can stake your life on, and we regularly do. When it comes to flying, does your cultural relativist bet his life on levitation or physics, a magic carpet or McDonnell Douglas? It doesn't matter which culture you were brought up in, Bernoulli's Principle[3] doesn't suddenly cease to operate as soon as you enter non-"Western" airspace. Or, where do you put your money when it comes to predicting an observation? Like a modern Rider Haggard hero, you can, as Carl Sagan pointed out, confound the savages of relativism and the New Age by predicting, to the second, a total eclipse of the sun a thousand years ahead.

Carl Sagan died a month ago. I met him once only, but I have loved his books, and I shall miss him as a "candle in the dark." I dedicate this lecture to his memory and shall use quotations from his writings. The remark about predicting eclipses is from the last book he published before he died, *The Demon-Haunted World*, and he went on:

> You can go to the witch doctor to lift the spell that causes your pernicious anaemia, or you can take vitamin B12. If you want to save your child from polio, you can pray or you can inoculate. If you're interested in the sex of

your unborn child, you can consult plumb-bob danglers all you want . . . but they'll be right, on average, only one time in two. If you want real accuracy . . . try amniocentesis and sonograms. Try science.[4]

Of course, scientists often disagree with one another. But they are proud to agree on what new evidence it would take to change their minds. The route to any discovery will be published, and whoever follows the same route should arrive at the same conclusion. If you lie—fiddle your figures, publish only that part of the evidence that supports your preferred conclusion—you will probably be found out. In any case, you won't get rich doing science, so why do it at all if you undermine the only point of the enterprise by lying? A scientist is much more likely to lie to a spouse or a tax inspector than to a scientific journal.

Admittedly, there are cases of fraud in science, and probably more than come to light. My claim is only that in the scientific community, fiddling data is the cardinal sin, unforgivable in a way that is hard to translate into the terms of another profession. An unfortunate consequence of this extreme value judgement is that scientists are exceptionally reluctant to blow the whistle on colleagues whom they may have reason to suspect of fiddling figures. It's rather like accusing somebody of cannibalism or paedophilia. Suspicions so dark may be suppressed until the evidence becomes too overwhelming to ignore, and by then much damage may have been done. If you fiddle your expense account, your peers will probably indulge you. If you pay a gardener in cash, thereby abetting a tax-dodging black market, you won't be a social pariah. But a scientist who is caught fiddling research data would be shunned and without mercy drummed out of the profession forever.

Barristers who use eloquence to make the best case they can, even if they don't believe it, even if they select favorable facts and slant the evidence, would be admired and rewarded for their success.[5] A scientist who does the same thing, pulling out all the rhetorical stops, twisting and turning every way to win support for a favorite theory, is regarded with at least mild suspicion.

Typically, the values of scientists are such that the charge of advocacy—or, worse, of being a *skilled* advocate—is a charge that needs to be answered.[6] But there is an important difference between using rhetoric to bring out what you believe is really there and using rhetoric knowingly to cover up what is really there. I once spoke in a university debate on evolution. The most effective creationist speech was made by a young woman who happened to be placed next to me at dinner afterwards. When I complimented her on her speech, she immediately told me she hadn't believed a word of it. She was simply exercising her debating skills by arguing passionately for the exact opposite of what she considered to be true. No doubt she will make a good lawyer. The fact that now it was all I could do to stay polite to my dinner companion may say something about the values that I have acquired as a scientist.

I suppose I am saying that scientists have a scale of values according to which there is something almost sacred about nature's truth. This may be why some of us get so heated about astrologers, spoonbenders, and similar charlatans, whom others indulgently tolerate as harmless entertainers.[7] The law of libel penalises those who knowingly tell lies about individuals. But you get off scot-free if you make money lying about nature—who can't sue. My values may be warped, but I'd like nature to enjoy the same rights of representation in court as does an abused child.[8]

The downside to the love of truth is that it may lead scientists to pursue it regardless of unfortunate consequences. Scientists do bear a heavy responsibility to warn society of those consequences. Einstein acknowledged the danger when he said, "If I had only known, I would have been a locksmith." But of course he wouldn't really. And when the opportunity came, he signed the famous letter alerting Roosevelt to the possibilities and dangers of the atomic bomb.[9]

Some of the hostility meted out to scientists is equivalent to shooting the messenger. If astronomers called our attention to a large asteroid on a collision course for earth, the final thought of many people before impact would be to blame "the scientists." There is an element of shooting the messenger about our reaction to bovine spongiform encephalitis (BSE). Unlike the asteroid case, here the true blame does belong with humanity. Scientists must bear some of it, along with the economic greed of the agricultural foodstuffs industry.

Carl Sagan remarks that he is often asked whether he believes there is intelligent life out there. He always leans towards a cautious yes but says it with humility and uncertainty:

> Often, I'm asked next, "What do you really think?"
> I say, "I just told you what I really think."
> "Yes, but what's your gut feeling?"
> But I try not to think with my gut. If I'm serious about understanding the world, thinking with anything besides my brain, as tempting as that might be, is likely to get me into trouble. Really, it's okay to reserve judgement until the evidence is in.[10]

Mistrust of inner, private revelation is, it seems to me, another of the values fostered by the experience of doing science. Private revelation doesn't sit well with the textbook ideals of scientific method: testability, evidential support, precision, quantifiability, consistency, intersubjectivity, repeatability, universality, and independence of cultural milieu.

There are also values of science which are probably best treated as being akin to aesthetic values. Einstein on the subject is sufficiently often quoted, so here, instead, is the great Indian astrophysicist Subrahmanyan Chandrasekhar, in a lecture in 1975, when he was sixty-five:

> In my entire scientific life . . . the most shattering experience has been the realisation that an exact solution of Einstein's equations of general relativity, discovered by the New Zealand mathematician Roy Kerr, provides the absolutely exact representation of untold numbers of massive black holes that populate the Universe. This "shuddering before the beautiful," this incredible fact that a discovery motivated by a search after the beautiful in mathematics should find its exact replica in Nature, persuades me to say that beauty is that to which the human mind responds at its deepest and most profound.[11]

I find this moving in a way that is missing from the skittish dilettantism of Keats's famous lines:

> "Beauty is truth, truth beauty,"—that is all
>   Ye know on earth, and all ye need to know.

Going only a little beyond aesthetics, scientists tend to value the long term at the expense of the short; they draw inspiration from the wide open spaces of the cosmos and the grinding slowness of geological time rather than the parochial concerns of humanity. They are especially prone to see things *sub specie aeternitatis* even if this puts them at risk of being accused of harboring a bleak, cold, unsympathetic view of humanity.

Carl Sagan's penultimate book, *Pale Blue Dot*, is built around the poetic image of our world seen from distant space:

> Look again at that dot. That's here. That's home.
>   The Earth is a very small stage in a vast cosmic arena. Think of the rivers of blood spilled by all those generals and emperors so that, in glory and triumph, they could become the momentary masters of a fraction of a dot. Think of the endless cruelties visited by the inhabitants of one corner of this pixel on the scarcely distinguishable inhabitants of some other corner, how frequent their misunderstandings, how eager they are to kill one another, how fervent their hatreds.
>   Our posturings, our imagined self-importance, the delusion that we have some privileged position in the Universe, are challenged by this point of pale light. Our planet is a lonely speck in a great enveloping cosmic dark. In our obscurity, in all this vastness, there is no hint that help will come from elsewhere to save us from ourselves.[12]

For me the only bleak aspect of this passage is the human realisation that its author is now silenced. Whether the scientific cutting down to size of humanity seems bleak is a matter of attitude. It may be an aspect of scientific values that many of us find such large visions uplifting and exhilarating rather than cold and empty.[13]

We also warm to nature as lawful and uncapricious. There is mystery but never magic, and mysteries are all the more beautiful for being eventually explained. Things are explicable, and it is our privilege to explain them. The principles that operate here prevail there—and "there" means out to distant galaxies. Charles Darwin, in the famous "entangled bank" passage which ends *The Origin of Species,* notes that all the complexity of life has "been produced by laws acting around us," and he goes on:

> Thus, from the war of nature, from famine and death, the most exalted object which we are capable of conceiving, namely, the production of the higher animals, directly follows. There is grandeur in this view of life, with its several powers, having been originally breathed into a few forms or into one; and that, whilst this planet has gone cycling on according to the fixed law of gravity, from so simple a beginning endless forms most beautiful and most wonderful have been, and are being, evolved.[14]

The sheer time it has taken species to evolve constitutes a favored argument for their conservation. This in itself involves a value judgement, presumably one congenial to those steeped in the depths of geological time. In a previous work, I have quoted Oria Douglas-Hamilton's harrowing account of an elephant cull in Zimbabwe:

> I looked at one of the discarded trunks and wondered how many millions of years it must have taken to create such a miracle of evolution. Equipped with fifty thousand muscles and controlled by a brain to match such complexity, it can wrench and push with tonnes of force . . . at the same time, it is capable of performing the most delicate operations. . . . And yet there it lay, amputated like so many elephant trunks I had seen all over Africa.[15]

Moving as this is, I quote it to illustrate the scientific values that led Douglas-Hamilton to stress the millions of years it has taken to evolve the complexity of an elephant's trunk rather than, say, the rights of elephants or their capacity to suffer or the value of wildlife in enriching our human experience or a country's tourist revenues.

Not that evolutionary understanding is irrelevant to questions of rights and suffering. I am shortly going to support the view that we cannot derive fundamental moral values from scientific knowledge. But utilitarian moral philosophers who do not believe there *are* any absolute moral values nevertheless justly claim a role in unmasking contradictions and inconsistencies within particular value systems.[16] Evolutionary scientists are well placed to observe inconsistencies in the absolutist elevation of human rights over those of all other species.

"Pro-lifers" assert, without question, that life is infinitely precious while cheerfully tucking into a large steak. The sort of "life" that such people are "pro" is all too clearly *human* life. Now, this is not necessarily wrong, but the evolutionary scientist will, at very least, warn us of inconsistency. It is not self-evident that abortion of a one-month human foetus is murder whereas shooting a fully sentient adult elephant or mountain gorilla is not.

Some 6 or 7 million years ago, there lived an African ape that was the common ancestor of all modern humans and all modern gorillas. By chance, the intermediate forms that link us to this ancestor—*Homo erectus, Homo habilis,* various members of the genus *Australopithecus,* and others—are extinct. Also extinct are the intermediates that link the same common ancestor to modern gorillas. If the intermediates were not extinct, if relict populations turned up in the jungles and savannahs of Africa, the consequences would be poignant. You'd be able to mate and have a child with someone, who'd be able to mate and have a child with someone else who . . . after a handful of further links in the chain, would be able to mate and have a child with a gorilla. It is sheer bad luck that some key intermediates in this chain of interfertility happen to be dead.[17]

This is not a frivolous thought-experiment. The only room for argument is over how many intermediate stages we need to postulate in the chain. And it doesn't matter how many intermediate stages there are in order to justify the following conclusion. Your absolutist elevation of *Homo sapiens* above all other species, your unargued preference for a human foetus or a brain-dead human vegetable over an adult chimpanzee at the height of its powers, your species-level apartheid, would collapse like a house of cards. Or if it did not, the comparison with apartheid would turn out to be no idle one. For if, in the face of a surviving continuum of intermediates, you insisted upon separating humans from non-humans, you could maintain the separation only by appealing to apartheidlike courts to decide whether particular intermediate individuals could "pass for human."

Such evolutionary logic does not destroy all doctrines of specifically human rights, but it certainly destroys absolutist versions, for it shows that the separation of our species depends upon accidents of extinction. If morals and rights were absolute in principle, they could not be jeopardised by new zoological discoveries in the Budongo Forest.

The Values of Science in the Strong Sense

I want to turn now from the weak to the strong sense of the values of science, to scientific findings as the direct source of a system of values. The versatile English biologist Sir Julian Huxley, incidentally a predecessor of mine as tutor in Zoology at New College, tried to make evolution the basis for an ethics, almost for a religion. For him, the Good is that which furthers the evolutionary process. His more distinguished but unknighted grandfather Thomas Henry Huxley took an almost opposite view. I am more in sympathy with Huxley senior.[18]

Part of Julian Huxley's ideological infatuation with evolution stemmed from his optimistic vision of its *progress*.[19] Nowadays it is fashionable to doubt that evolution really is progressive at all. This is an interesting argument, and I have a view on it,[20] but it is superseded by the prior question of whether we should anyway base our values upon this or any other conclusion about nature.

A similar point arises about Marxism. You can espouse an academic theory of history that predicts the dictatorship of the proletariat, and you can follow a political creed that values the dictatorship of the proletariat as a good thing that you should work to engage. As a matter of fact, many Marxists do both, and like Marx himself, a disconcerting number cannot tell the difference. But logically, the political belief in what is desirable does not follow from the academic theory of history. You could consistently be an academic Marxist believing that the forces of history drive inexorably towards a workers' revolution, while at the same time voting High Tory and working as hard as possible to postpone the inevitable. Or you could be a passionate Marxist politically, who works all the harder for the revolution precisely because you doubt the Marxist theory of history and feel that the longed-for revolution needs all the help it can get.

Similarly, evolution may or may not have the quality of progressiveness that Julian Huxley, as an academic biologist, supposed. But whether he was right or not about the biology, it clearly is not necessary that we should imitate this kind of progressiveness in drawing up our systems of values.

The issue is even starker if we move from evolution itself, with its alleged progressive momentum, to Darwin's mechanism of evolution, the survival of the fittest. T. H. Huxley, in his Romanes Lecture, was under no illusions, and he was right.[21] If you must use Darwinism as a morality play, it is an awful warning. Nature really is red in tooth and claw. The weakest really do go to the wall, and natural selection really does favor selfish genes. The racing elegance of cheetahs and gazelles is bought at huge cost in blood and the suffering of countless antecedents on both sides. Ancient antelopes were butchered and carnivores starved, in the shaping of their streamlined modern counterparts. The product of natural selection, life in all its forms, is beautiful and rich. But the process is vicious, brutal, and short-sighted.[22]

As an academic fact we are Darwinian creatures, our forms and our brains sculpted by natural selection, that indifferent, cruelly blind watchmaker. But this doesn't mean we have to like it. On the contrary, a Darwinian society is not the sort of society in which any friend of mine would wish to live. "Darwinian" is not a bad definition of precisely the sort of politics I would run a hundred miles not to be governed by, a sort of over-the-top Thatcherism gone native.

I should be allowed a personal word here because I am tired of being identified with a vicious politics of ruthless competitiveness, accused of advancing selfishness as a way of life.[23] Soon after Margaret Thatcher's election victory of 1979, Steven Rose wrote in *New Scientist* as follows:

> I am not implying that Saatchi and Saatchi engaged a team of sociobiologists to write the Thatcher scripts, nor even that certain Oxford and Sussex dons are beginning to rejoice at this practical expression of the simple truths of selfish genery they have been struggling to convey to us. The coincidence of fashionable theory with political events is messier than that. I do believe though, that when the history of the move to the right of the late 1970s comes to be written, from law and order to monetarism and to the (more contradictory) attack on statism, then the switch in scientific fashion, if only from group to kin selection models in evolutionary theory, will come to be seen as part of the tide which has rolled the Thatcherites and their concept of a fixed, 19th century competitive and xenophobic human nature into power.[24]

The "Sussex don" referred to was John Maynard Smith, and he gave the apt reply in a letter to the next issue of *New Scientist:* what should we have done, fiddled the equations?

Rose was a leader of the Marxist-inspired attack of the time on sociobiology.[25] It is entirely typical that, just as these Marxists were incapable of separating their academic theory of history from their normative political beliefs, they assumed that we were incapable of separating our biology from our politics. They simply could not grasp that one might hold academic beliefs about the way evolution happens in nature while simultaneously repudiating the desirability of translating those academic beliefs into politics. This led them to the untenable conclusion that, since genetic Darwinism when applied to humans had undesirable political connotations, it must not be *allowed* to be scientifically correct.

They and many others make the same kind of mistake with respect to positive eugenics. The premise is that to breed humans selectively for abilities such as running speed, musical talent, or mathematical dexterity would be politically and morally indefensible. Therefore it isn't (*must* not be) possible—ruled out by science. Well, anybody can see that that's a non sequitur, and I'm sorry to have to tell you that positive eugenics is not ruled out by science. There is no reason to doubt that humans would respond to selective breeding just as readily as cows, dogs, cereal plants, and chickens. I hope it isn't necessary for me to say that this doesn't mean I am in favor of it.

There are those who will accept the feasibility of physical eugenics but dig their trench before mental eugenics. Maybe you could breed a race of Olympic swimming champions, they concede, but you will never breed for higher intelligence, either because there's no agreed method of measuring intelligence, or because intelligence is not a single quantity varying in one dimension, or because intelligence doesn't vary genetically, or some combination of these three points.

If you seek refuge in any of these lines of thought, it is once again my unpleasant duty to disillusion you. It doesn't matter if we can't agree how to measure intelligence; we can breed for any of the disputed measures, or a combination of them. It might be hard agreeing upon a definition for docility in dogs, but this doesn't stop us breeding for it. It doesn't matter if intelligence is not a single variable; the same is probably true of milking prowess in cows and racing ability in horses. You can still breed for them, even while disputing how they should be measured, or whether they each constitute a single dimension of variation.

As for the suggestion that intelligence, measured in any way or in any combination of ways, does not vary genetically—it more or less cannot be true, for the following reason whose logic requires only the premiss that we are more intelligent—by whatever definition you choose—than chimpanzees and all other apes. If we are more intelligent than the ape that lived 6 million years ago and was our common ancestor with chimpanzees, there has been an evolutionary trend in our ancestry towards increased intelligence. There has certainly been an evolutionary trend towards increased brain size: it is one of the more dramatic evolutionary trends in the vertebrate fossil record. Evolutionary trends cannot happen unless there is genetic variation in the characteristics concerned—in this case brain size and presumably intelligence. So, there was genetic variation in intelligence in our ancestors. It is just possible that there isn't any longer, but such an exceptional circumstance would be bizarre. Even if the evidence from twin studies did not support it—which it does—we could safely draw the conclusion, from evolutionary logic alone, that we have genetic variance in intelligence, intelligence being defined in terms of whatever separates us from our ape ancestors. Using the same definition, we could, if we wanted to, use artificial selective breeding to continue the same evolutionary trend.

I would need little persuading that such a eugenic policy would be politically and morally wrong, but we must be absolutely clear that such a *value judgement* is the right reason to refrain from it. Let us not allow our value judgements to push us over into the false scientific belief that human eugenics isn't *possible*. Nature, fortunately, is indifferent to anything so parochial as human values.

Later, Rose joined forces with Leon Kamin, one of America's leading opponents of IQ-measuring and with the distinguished Marxist geneticist Richard Lewontin, to write a book in which they repeated these and many other errors. They also acknowledged that the sociobiologists wanted to be less fascist than our science, in their (mistaken) view, ought to make us, but they (equally mistakenly) tried to catch us in a contradiction with the mechanistic interpretation of mind that we—and they—purport to follow:

> Such a position is, or ought to be, completely in accord with the principles of sociobiology offered by Wilson and Dawkins. However, to adopt it would involve them in the dilemma of first arguing the innateness of much human behavior that, being liberal men, they clearly find unattractive (spite, indoctrination, etc.) . . . To avoid this problem, Wilson and Dawkins invoke a free will that enables us to go against the dictates of our genes if we so wish.[26]

This, they complain, is a return to unabashed Cartesian dualism. You cannot, say Rose and his colleagues, believe that we are survival machines programmed by our genes and at the same time urge rebellion against them.

What's the problem? Without going into the difficult philosophy of determinism and free will, it is easy to observe that, as a matter of fact, we do go against the dictates of our genes.[27] We rebel every time we use contraception when we'd be economically capable of rearing a child. We rebel when we give lectures, write books, or compose sonatas instead of single-mindedly devoting our time and energy to disseminating our genes.

This is easy stuff; there is no philosophical difficulty at all. Natural selection of selfish genes gave us big brains which were originally useful for survival in a purely utilitarian sense. Once those big brains, with their linguistic and other capacities, were in place, there is no contradiction at all in saying that they took off in wholly new "emergent" directions, including directions opposed to the interests of selfish genes.

There is nothing self-contradictory about emergent properties. Electronic computers, conceived as calculating machines, emerge as word processors, chess players, encyclopaedias, telephone switchboards, and even, I regret to say, electronic horoscopes. No fundamental contradictions are there to ring philosophic alarm bells, or in the statement that our brains have overtaken, even overreached, their Darwinian provenance. Just as we defy our selfish genes when we wantonly detach the enjoyment of sex from its Darwinian function, so we can sit down together and with language devise politics, ethics, and values that are vigorously anti-Darwinian in their thrust. I shall return to this in my conclusion.

One of Hitler's perverted sciences was a garbled Darwinism and, of course, eugenics. But, uncomfortable though it is to admit it, Hitler's views were not unusual in the first part of this century. I quote from a chapter on the "New Republic," an allegedly Darwinian utopia, written in 1902:

> And how will the New Republic treat the inferior races? How will it deal with the black? . . . the yellow man? . . . the Jew? . . . those swarms of black, and brown, and dirty-white, and yellow people, who do not come into the new needs of efficiency? Well, the world is a world, and not a charitable institution, and I take it they will have to go.

The author of this is H. G. Wells, who thought of himself as a socialist. Equally shocking to modern minds is the gusto with which Wells sets out the practical methods by which his "men of the New Republic" will take the Darwinian law into their hands:

> And the ethical system of these men of the New Republic, the ethical system which will dominate the world state, will be shaped primarily to favor the procreation of what is fine and efficient and beautiful in humanity—beautiful and strong bodies, clear and powerful minds. . . . And the method that nature has followed hitherto in the shaping of the world, whereby weakness was prevented from propagating weakness . . . is death. . . . The men of the New Republic . . . will have an ideal that will make the killing worth the while.[28]

It is stuff like this (and there's lots more from the Social Darwinists) that has given Darwinism a bad name in the social sciences. And how! But, again, we must not attempt to use the facts of nature to derive our politics or our morality one way or the other. David Hume is to be preferred to either of the two Huxleys: moral directives cannot be derived from descriptive premises, or, as it is more colloquially put, "You can't get an 'ought' from an 'is.'" Where then, on the evolutionary view, do our "oughts" come from? Where do we get our values, moral and aesthetic, ethical and political? It is time to move on from the values of science to the science of values.

The Science of Values

Have we inherited our values from remote ancestors? The onus is on those who would deny it. The tree of life, Darwin's tree, is a vast, bushy thicket of 30 million twigs. We are one tiny twig, buried somewhere in the surface layers. Our twig sprouts from a small bough alongside our ape cousins, not far from the larger bough of our monkey cousins, within view of our more distant cousins, cousin kangaroo, cousin octopus, cousin staphylococcus. Nobody doubts that all the rest of the 30 million twigs inherit their attributes from their ancestors, and by any standards we humans owe to our ancestors much of what we are and what we look like. We have inherited from our forebears—with greater or less modification—our bones and eyes, our ears and thighs, even, it is hard to doubt, our lusts and our fears. A priori there seems no obvious reason why the same should not apply to our higher mental faculties, our arts and our morals, our sense of natural justice, our values. Can we exclude these manifestations of high humanity from what Darwin called the indelible stamp of our lowly origins?[29] Or was Darwin right when he remarked more informally to himself in one of his notebooks, "He who understands baboon would do more towards metaphysics than Locke"?[30] I shall make no attempt to review the literature, but the question of the Darwinian evolution of values and morals has been frequently and extensively discussed.[31]

Here's the fundamental logic of Darwinism. Everybody has ancestors, but not everybody has descendants. We have all inherited the genes for being an ancestor, at the expense of the genes for failing to be an ancestor. Ancestry is the ultimate Darwinian value. In a purely Darwinian world, all other values are subsidiary. Synonymously, gene survival is the ultimate Darwinian value. As a first expectation, all animals and plants can be expected to work ceaselessly for the long-term survival of the genes that ride inside them.

The world is divided into those for whom the simple logic of this is as clear as daylight, and those who, no matter how many times it is explained to them, just don't get it. Alfred Wallace wrote about the problem in a letter to his co-discoverer of natural selection: "My dear Darwin—I have been so repeatedly struck by the utter inability of numbers of intelligent persons to see clearly, or at all, the self-acting and necessary effects of natural selection."[32] Those who don't get it either assume that there must be some kind of personal agent in the background to do the choosing, or they wonder why individuals should value survival of their own genes, rather than, for instance, the survival of their species or the survival of the ecosystem of which they are a part. After all, say this second group of people, if the species and the ecosystem don't survive, neither will the individuals, so it is in their interests to value the species and the ecosystem. Who decides, they wonder, that gene survival is the ultimate value?

Nobody decides. It follows automatically from the fact that genes reside in the bodies that they build and are the only things (in the form of coded copies) that reliably persist from one generation of bodies to the next. This is the modern version of the point Wallace was making with his apt phrase "self-acting." Individuals are not miraculously or cognitively inspired with values and goals that will guide them in the paths of gene survival. Only the past can have an influence, not the future. Animals behave *as if* striving for the future values of the selfish gene simply and solely because they bear, and are influenced by, genes that survived through ancestral generations in the past. Those ancestors that, in their own time, behaved as if they valued whatever was conducive to the future survival of their genes have bequeathed those very genes to their descendants. So their descendants behave as if they, in their turn, value the future survival of their genes.

It is an entirely unpremeditated, self-acting process which works so long as future conditions are tolerably similar to past. If they are not, it doesn't, and the result is often extinction. Those that understand this understand Darwinism. The word Darwinism, by the way, was coined by the ever-generous Wallace.[33] I shall continue my Darwinian analysis of values using bones as my example, because they are unlikely to ruffle human hackles and therefore distract.

Bones are not perfect; they sometimes break. A wild animal that breaks its leg is unlikely to survive in the harsh, competitive world of nature. It will be especially vulnerable to predators or unable to catch prey. So why doesn't natural selection thicken bones so that they never break? We humans, by artificial selection, could breed a race of, say, dogs whose leg bones were so stout that they never broke. Why doesn't nature do the same? Because of costs, and this implies a system of values.

Engineers and architects are never asked to build unbreakable structures or impregnable walls. Instead, they are given a monetary budget and asked to do the best they can, according to certain criteria, within that constraint. Or, they may be told, "The bridge must bear a weight of 10 tons and must withstand gales three times more forceful than the worst ever recorded in this gorge. Now design the cheapest bridge you can that meets these specifications." Safety factors in engineering imply monetary valuation of human life. Designers of civilian airliners are more risk-averse than designers of military aircraft. All aircraft and ground control facilities could be safer if more money was spent. More redundancy could be built into control systems; the number of flying hours demanded of pilots before they are allowed to carry live passengers could be increased. Baggage inspection could be more stringent and time consuming.

The reason we don't take these steps to make life safer is largely one of cost. We are prepared to pay a lot of money, time, and trouble for human safety, but not infinite amounts. Like it or not, we are forced to put monetary value on human life. In most people's scale of values, human life rates higher than nonhuman animal life, but animal life does not have zero value. Notoriously, the evidence of newspaper coverage suggests that people value life belonging to their own race higher than human life generally. In wartime, both absolute and relative valuations of human life change dramatically. People who think it is somehow wicked to talk about this monetary valuation of human life—people who emotionally declare that a single human life has infinite value—are living in cloud-cuckooland. Darwinian selection, too, optimises within economic limits and can be said to have values in the same sense. John Maynard Smith suggested that if there were no constraints on what is possible, the best phenotype would live forever, would be impregnable to predators, would lay eggs at an infinite rate, and so on.[34] Nicholas Humphrey continued the argument with another analogy from engineering:

> Henry Ford, it is said, commissioned a survey of the car scrapyards of America to find out if there were parts of the Model T Ford which never failed. His inspectors came back with reports of almost every kind of breakdown: axles, brakes, piston—all were liable to go wrong. But they drew attention to one notable exception, the *kingpins* of the scrapped cars invariably had years of life left in them. With ruthless logic Ford concluded that the kingpins on the Model T were too good for their job and ordered that in future they should be made to an inferior specification. . . . Nature is surely at least as careful an economist as Henry Ford.[35]

Humphrey applied his lesson to the evolution of intelligence, but it can equally be applied to bones or anything else. Let us commission a survey of the corpses of gibbons to see if there are some bones that never fail. We find that every bone in the body breaks at one time or another, with one notable exception: let's say the femur (thigh bone) is never known to break. Henry Ford would be in no doubt. In future, the femur must be made to an inferior specification.

Natural selection would agree. Individuals with slightly thinner femurs who diverted the material saved into some other purpose, say building up other bones and making them less likely to break, would survive better. Or females might take the calcium shaved off the thickness of the femur and put it into milk, thereby improving the survival of their offspring—and with them the genes for making the economy.

In a machine or an animal the (simplified) ideal is that all the parts should wear out simultaneously. If there is one part that consistently has years of life left in it after the others have worn out, it is overdesigned. Materials that went into building it up should, instead, be diverted to other parts. If there is one part that consistently wears out before anything else, it is underdesigned. It should be built up using materials taken away from other parts. Natural selection will tend to uphold an equilibration rule: "Rob from strong bones to pay weak ones, until all are of equal strength."

The reason this is a slight oversimplification is that not all the bits of an animal or a machine are equally important. That's why in-flight entertainment systems go wrong, thankfully, more often than rudders or jet engines. A gibbon might be able to afford a broken femur better than a broken humerus. Its way of life depends upon "brachiation" (swinging through the trees by its arms). A gibbon with a broken leg might survive to have another child. A gibbon with a broken arm probably wouldn't. So the equilibration rule I mentioned has to be tempered: "Rob from strong bones to pay weak ones, until you have equalised the risks to your survival accruing from breakages in all parts of your skeleton."

But who is the "you" admonished in the equilibration rule? It certainly isn't an individual gibbon, who is not, we assume, capable of making compensatory adjustments to its own bones. The "you" is an abstraction. You can think of it as a lineage of gibbons in ancestor/descendant relation to one another, represented by the genes that they share. As the lineage progresses, ancestors whose genes make the right adjustments survive to leave descendants who inherit those correctly equilibrating genes. The genes that we see in the world tend to be the ones that get the equilibration right, because they have survived through a long line of successful ancestors who have not suffered the breakage of underdesigned, or the waste of overdesigned, bones.

So much for bones. Now we need to establish, in Darwinian terms, what values are doing for animals and plants. Where bones stiffen limbs, what do values do for their possessors? By values, I am now going to mean the criteria, in the brain, by which animals choose how to behave.

The majority of things in the universe don't actively strive for anything. They just are. I am concerned with the minority that do strive for things, entities that appear to work towards some end and then stop when they've achieved it. This minority I shall call value driven. Some of them are animals and plants, some manmade machines. Thermostats, heat-seeking Sidewinder missiles, and numerous physiological systems in animals and plants are controlled by negative feedback. There is a target value defined in the system. Discrepancies from the target value are sensed and fed back into the system, causing it to change its state in the direction of reducing the discrepancy.

Other value-seeking systems improve with experience. From the point of view of defining values in learning systems, the key concept is *reinforcement*. Reinforcers are positive ("rewards") or negative ("punishments"). Rewards are states of the world which, when encountered, cause an animal to repeat whatever it recently did. Punishments are states of the world which, when encountered, cause an animal to avoid repeating whatever it recently did.

The stimuli that animals treat as rewards and punishments are primitive values. Psychologists make a further distinction between primary and secondary reinforcers (both rewards and punishments). Chimpanzees learn to work for food as a primary reward, but they will also learn to work for the equivalent of money—secondary rewards—plastic tokens which they have previously learned to stuff into a slot machine to get food.

Some theorists have argued that there is only one primary built-in reward ("drive reduction" or "need reduction") upon which all others are built. Others, such as Konrad Lorenz, the grand old man of ethology, argued that Darwinian natural selection has built-in complicated rewarding mechanisms, specified differently and in detail for each species to fit its unique way of life.[36]

Perhaps the most elaborately detailed examples of primary values come from birdsong.[37] Different species develop their songs in different ways. The American song sparrow is a fascinating mixture. Young birds brought up completely alone end up singing normal song sparrow song. So, unlike, say, bullfinches, they don't learn by imitation. But they do learn. Young song sparrows teach themselves to sing by babbling at random and repeating those fragments that match a built-in template. The template is a genetically specified preconception of what a song sparrow ought to sound like. You could say that the information is built in by the genes, but into the sensory part of the brain. It has to be transferred to the motor side by learning. And the sensation specified by the template, by definition, is a reward: the bird repeats actions that deliver it. But, as rewards go, it is very elaborate and precisely specified in detail.

It is examples like this that stimulated Lorenz to use the colorful phrase "innate schoolmarm" (or "innate teaching mechanism") in his lengthy attempts to resolve the ancient dispute over nativism versus environmentalism. His point was that, however important learning is, there has to be innate guidance of what we learn. In particular, each species needs to be supplied with its own specifications of what to treat as rewarding and what as punishing. *Primary* values, Lorenz was saying, have to come from Darwinian natural selection.

Given enough time, we should be able to breed, by artificial selection, a race of animals that enjoy pain and hate pleasure. Of course, by the animals' newly evolved definition, this statement is oxymoronic. I'll rephrase it. By artificial selection, we could reverse the previous definitions of pleasure and pain.[38]

The animals so modified will be less well equipped to survive than their wild ancestors. Wild ancestors have been naturally selected to enjoy those stimuli most likely to improve their survival and to treat as painful those stimuli most likely, statistically, to kill them. Injuring the body, puncturing skin, breaking bones—all are perceived as painful for good Darwinian reasons. Our artificially selected animals will enjoy having their skin pierced, will actively seek to break their own bones, and will bask in a temperature so hot or so cold as to endanger their survival.

Similar artificial selection would work with humans. Not only could you breed for tastes, you could breed for callousness, sympathy, loyalty, slothfulness, piety, meanness, or the Protestant work ethic. This is a less radical claim than it sounds, for genes don't fix behavior deterministically; they only contribute quantitatively to statistical tendencies. Nor, as we saw when discussing the values of science, does this possibility imply a single gene for each of these complicated things, any more than the feasibility of breeding racehorses implies a single gene for speed. In the absence of artificial breeding, our own values are presumably influenced by natural selection under conditions that prevailed during the Pleistocene era in Africa.

Humans are unique in many ways. Perhaps our most obviously unique feature is language. Whereas eyes have evolved between forty and sixty times independently around the animal kingdom,[39] language has evolved only once. It seems learned, but there is strong genetic supervision of the learning process. The particular language that we speak is learned, but the tendency to learn *language* rather than just any old thing is inherited and evolved specifically in our human line. We also inherit evolved rules for grammar. The exact readout of these rules varies from language to language, but their deep structure is laid down by the genes and is presumably evolved by natural selection just as surely as our lusts and our bones. Evidence is good that the brain contains a language "module," a computational mechanism that actively seeks to learn language and actively uses grammatical rules to structure it.[40]

According to the young and thriving discipline of evolutionary psychology, the language learning module stands as exemplar of a whole set of inherited, special-purpose computational modules. We might expect modules for sex and reproduction, for analysing kinship (important for doling out altruism and avoiding dysgenic incest), for counting debts and policing obligations, for judging fairness and natural justice, perhaps for throwing projectiles accurately towards a distant target, and for classifying useful animals and plants. These modules will presumably be mediated by specific, built-in values.[41]

If we turn Darwinian eyes on our modern, civilised selves and our predilections—our aesthetic values, our capacity for pleasure—it is important to wear sophisticated spectacles. Do not ask how a middle manager's ambitions for a bigger desk and a softer office carpet benefit his selfish genes. Ask, instead, how these urban partialities might stem from a mental module that was selected to do something else, in a different place and time. For office carpet, perhaps (and I mean *perhaps*), read soft and warm animal skins whose possession betokened hunting success. The whole art of applying Darwinian thinking to modern, domesticated humanity is to discern the correct rewriting rules. Take your question about the foibles of civilised, urban humanity and rewrite it back half a million years and out onto the African plains.

Evolutionary psychologists have coined the term "environment of evolutionary adaptedness" (EEA) for that set of conditions in which our wild ancestors evolved. There's a lot that we don't know about the EEA; the fossil record is limited. Some of what we guess about it comes, through a kind of reverse engineering, from examining ourselves and trying to work out the kind of environment to which our attributes would have been well adapted.

We know that the EEA was located in Africa, probably, though not certainly, on scrubby savannah. It is plausible that our ancestors lived in these conditions as hunter-gatherers, perhaps in something like the way modern hunter-gatherer tribes live but, at least in earlier periods, with a less-developed technology. We know that fire was tamed more than a million years ago by *Homo erectus,* the species that was probably our immediate predecessor in evolution. It is controversial when our ancestors dispersed out of Africa. We know that there were *Homo erectus* in Asia a million years ago, but many believe that nobody today is descended from them and that all surviving humans are the descendants of a second, more recent exodus of *Homo sapiens* out of Africa.[42]

Whenever the exodus, there has evidently been time for humans to adapt to non-African conditions. Arctic humans are different from tropical ones. We northerners have lost the black pigmentation that our African ancestors presumably had. There has been time for biochemistries to diverge in response to diet. Some peoples—perhaps those with herding traditions—retain into adulthood the ability to digest lactose. In other peoples, only children can digest milk; the adults suffer from the condition known as lactose intolerance. Presumably the differences have evolved by natural selection in different culturally determined environments. If natural selection has had time to shape our bodies and our biochemistry since some of us left Africa, it should also have had time to shape our brains and our values. So we needn't necessarily pay total heed to specifically African aspects of the EEA. Nevertheless, the genus *Homo* has spent at least nine-tenths of its time in Africa, and the hominids have spent 99 percent of their time in Africa, so, insofar as our values are inherited from our ancestors, we might still expect a substantial African influence.

Various researchers, most notably Gordon Orians of the University of Washington, have examined aesthetic preferences for various kinds of landscapes.[43] What kinds of environments do we seek to re-create in our gardens? These workers try to relate the sorts of places we find attractive to the sorts of places that our wild ancestors would have encountered as nomads wandering from campsite to campsite in the EEA. For example, we might be expected to like trees of the genus *Acacia* or other trees that resemble them. We might prefer landscapes in which the trees were low and dotted about to deep forest landscapes or deserts, both of which might carry threatening messages for us.

Moving to more detail, *given* that we are looking at a landscape resembling the African savannah, are we attracted by those features that distinguish a promising environment from an ominous one? An important virtue of a good campsite is the presence of water. Could this be why everybody loves a stream or pond in their garden, and why so many of us claim to be lulled to sleep by the reassuring sound of running water?

In one study, subjects drawn from six age groups were shown slides of five natural biomes and asked which they would prefer to "visit" or "live in." The five biomes on offer were tropical forest, deciduous forest, coniferous forest, East African savannah, and desert. The authors think it significant that small children preferred the East African savannah slides. Older subjects showed more varied tastes, suggesting, to the authors, that learned preferences had replaced the inherited one. It seems to me unfortunate that the experimenters did not offer mountain scenes or seascapes, both favorite holiday environments, which might well have been preferred to the East African savannah scenes. Omissions like this are unfortunate because they prompt suspicions of special pleading and lack of objectivity in the experimental design.

Special pleading, too, might be a fair accusation to level against the following:

> For an organism that rarely eats flowers, it is perhaps surprising that we place such a high value on them and spend so much effort and money to have flowers in and around our dwellings and in city parks. The evolutionary biologist, however, sees flowers as signals of improving resources and as providing cues about good foraging sites some time in the future.[44]

Well, maybe. But I can't help reflecting that, if people *did* eat flowers, the simpler explanation would have sufficed and the more indirect one would not even have been mentioned. We must be constantly alive to the accusation of explaining, with post hoc facility, whatever facts nature throws at us. Of course this complaint doesn't always mean that the special pleading leads to the wrong answer.

There seem to be some grounds for suspicion of this kind of work. Less justified would be a general scepticism that anything so complex or high-flown as preference for a landscape could possibly be programmed into the genes. On the contrary, there is nothing intrinsically implausible about such values being inherited. Once again, a sexual parallel comes to mind. The act of sexual intercourse, if we contemplate it dispassionately, is pretty bizarre. The idea that there could be genes "for" enjoying this preposterously unlikely act of rhythmic insertion and withdrawal might strike us as implausible in the extreme. But it is inescapable if we accept that sexual desire has evolved by Darwinian selection. Darwinian selection can't work if there are no genes to select. And if we can inherit genes for enjoying penile insertion, there is nothing inherently implausible in the idea that we could inherit genes for admiring certain landscapes, enjoying certain kinds of music, hating the taste of mangoes, or anything else.

Fear of heights, manifesting itself in vertigo and in the common dreams of falling, might well be natural in species that spend a good deal of their time in trees, as our ancestors did. Fear of spiders, snakes, and scorpions might with benefit be built into any African species. If you have a nightmare about snakes, it is just possible that you are not dreaming about symbolic phalluses but actually about *snakes*. Biologists have often noted that phobic reactions are commonly exhibited toward spiders and snakes, almost never to electric bulb sockets and motor cars. Yet in our temperate and urban world, snakes and spiders no longer constitute a source of danger, whereas electric sockets and cars are potentially lethal.[45]

To take another example, it is notoriously hard to persuade drivers to slow down in fog or refrain from tailgating at high speed. The economist Armen Alchian ingeniously suggested abolishing seatbelts and compulsorily fixing a sharp spear to all cars, pointing from the centre of the steering wheel straight at the driver's heart.[46] I think I'd find it persuasive, but whether for atavistic reasons I don't know. Also persuasive is the following calculation. If a car travelling at 80 miles per hour is abruptly slammed to a halt, this is equivalent to hitting the ground after falling from a tall building. In other words, when you are driving fast, it is as if you were hanging from the top of a high-rise building by a rope sufficiently thin that its probability of breaking is equal to the probability that the driver in front of you will do something really stupid. I know almost nobody who could happily sit on a windowsill up a skyscraper and few who unequivocally enjoy bungee jumping. Yet almost everybody happily travels at high speed along motorways, even if they clearly understand in a cerebral way the danger they are in. I think it is quite plausible that we are genetically programmed to be afraid of heights and sharp points but that we have to learn (and are not very good at it) to be afraid of travelling at high speeds.

Social habits that are universal among all peoples, such as laughing, smiling, weeping, believing in God, and having a statistical tendency to avoid incest, are likely to have been present in our common ancestors too. Hans Hass and Irenaeus Eibl-Eibesfeldt travelled the world clandestinely, filming people's facial expressions, and concluded that there are cross-cultural universals in styles of flirting, of threatening, and in a fairly complicated repertoire of facial expressions.[47] They filmed one child born blind whose smile and other expressions of emotion were normal although she had never seen another face.

Children notoriously have a highly developed sense of natural justice, and "not fair" is one of the first expressions to spring to the lips of a disgruntled child. This does not, of course, show that a sense of fairness is universally built in by the genes, but some might consider it suggestive in the same kind of way as the smile of the child born blind. It would be tidy if different cultures, the world over, shared the same ideas of natural justice, but there are some disconcerting differences. Most people attending this lecture would think it unjust to punish an individual for the crimes of his grandfather. Yet there are cultures in which the vendetta is taken for granted and is presumably regarded as naturally just. This perhaps suggests that, at least in detail, our sense of natural justice is pretty flexible and variable.

Continuing our guesswork about our ancestors' world, the EEA, there are reasons to think that they lived in stable bands, either roving and foraging like modern baboons, or perhaps more settled, in villages like present-day hunter-gatherers such as the Yanomamö of the Amazon jungle.[48] In either case, stability of grouping means that individuals would tend to encounter the same individuals repeatedly throughout their lives. Seen through Darwinian eyes, this could have had important consequences for the evolution of our values. In particular, it might help us to understand why, from the point of view of our selfish genes, we are so absurdly nice to each other.

It is not quite as absurd as it might naively appear. Genes may be selfish, but this is far from saying that individual organisms must be hard and selfish. A large purpose of the doctrine of the selfish gene is to explain how selfishness at the gene level can lead to altruism at the level of the individual organism. But this explanation covers altruism only as a kind of selfishness in disguise: first, altruism towards kin (nepotism); and second, boons given in the mathematical expectation of reciprocation (you help me, and I'll repay you later).

This is where our assumption of life in villages or tribal bands can help, in two ways. First, there would probably have been a degree of inbreeding, as my colleague W. D. Hamilton has argued. Although, like many other mammals, humans go out of their way to combat the extremes of inbreeding, nevertheless, neighboring tribes frequently speak mutually unintelligible languages and practice incompatible religions, which inevitably limits crossbreeding. Assuming various low rates of between-village migration, Hamilton calculated the expected levels of genetic resemblance within tribes as compared with between tribes. His conclusion was that, under plausible assumptions, fellow village members might as well be brothers by comparison with outsiders from other villages.[49]

Such conditions in the EEA would tend to favor xenophobia: "Be unpleasant to strangers not from your own village, because strangers are statistically unlikely to share the same genes." It is too simple to conclude that, conversely, natural selection in tribal villages would necessarily have favored general altruism: "Be nice to anyone you meet, because anyone you meet is statistically likely to share your genes for general altruism." But there could be additional conditions in which the latter would indeed be so, and this was Hamilton's conclusion.

The other consequence of the village pattern follows from the theory of reciprocal altruism, which received a fillip in 1984 from the publication of Robert Axelrod's book, *The Evolution of Cooperation.* Axelrod took the theory of games, specifically the game of prisoner's dilemma, and, abetted by Hamilton, thought about it in an evolutionary way, using simple but ingenious computer models. His work has become well known, and I shan't describe it in detail but summarise some relevant conclusions.[50]

In an evolutionary world of fundamentally selfish entities, those individuals that cooperate turn out to be surprisingly likely to prosper. The cooperation is not based upon indiscriminate trust but upon swift identification and vigorous punishing of defection. Axelrod coined a measure, the "Shadow of the Future," for how far ahead, on average, individuals can expect to go on meeting. If the shadow of the future is short or if individual identification or its equivalent is hard, mutual trust is unlikely to develop, and universal defection becomes the rule. If the shadow of the future is long, relationships of initial trust, tempered by suspicion of betrayal, are likely to develop. Such would have been the case in the EEA if our speculations about tribal villages or roving bands are correct. Therefore we might expect to find in ourselves deep-seated tendencies towards what may be called "suspicious trust."

We should also expect to find in ourselves special-purpose brain modules for calculating debt and repayment, for reckoning who owes how much to whom, for feeling pleased when one gains (but perhaps even more displeased when one loses), and for mediating the sense of natural justice that I have already mentioned.

Axelrod went on to apply his version of game theory to the special case in which individuals bear conspicuous labels. Suppose the population contains two types, arbitrarily called the reds and the greens. Axelrod concluded that, under plausible conditions, a strategy of the following form would be evolutionarily stable: "If red, be nice to reds but nasty to greens; if green, be nice to greens but nasty to reds." This follows regardless of the actual nature of redness and greenness and regardless of whether the two types differ in any other respect at all.[51] So, superimposed over the "suspicious trust" I have mentioned, we should not be surprised to see discrimination of this kind.

What might "red" versus "green" correspond to in real life? Plausibly, it may mean own tribe versus other tribe. We have reached, via a different theory, the same conclusion as Hamilton with his inbreeding calculations. So, the "village model" leads us, by two quite distinct lines of theory, to expect in-group altruism jockeying with tendencies to xenophobia.

Now, selfish genes are not conscious little agents, taking decisions for their own future good. The genes that survive are the ones that wired up ancestral brains with appropriate rules of thumb, actions that had the consequence, in ancestral environments, of assisting survival and reproduction. Since our modern urban environment is so different, the genes cannot be expected to adjust—there hasn't been time for the slow process of natural selection to catch up. The same rules of thumb will be acted out as if nothing had happened. From the selfish genes' point of view, this is a mistake, like our love of sugar in a modern world where sugar is no longer scarce and rots our teeth. It is entirely to be expected that there should be such mistakes. Perhaps, when you pity and help a beggar in the street, you are the misfiring instrument of a Darwinian rule of thumb set up in a tribal past when things were very different. I hasten to add that I use the word "misfiring" in a strictly Darwinian sense, not as an expression of my own values.

So far so good, but there is probably more to goodness than the preceding explanation indicates. Many of us seem generous beyond what would pay on "selfishness in disguise" grounds, even assuming that we once lived in inbred bands who could expect a lifetime of opportunities for mutual repayment. If I live in such a world, I shall ultimately benefit if I build up a reputation for trustworthiness, for being the kind of person with whom you can enter into a bargain without fear of betrayal. As my colleague Matt Ridley puts it in his admirable book *The Origins of Virtue*: "Now, suddenly, there is a new and powerful reason to be nice: to persuade people to play with you."[52] He quotes the economist Robert Frank's experimental evidence that people are good at rapidly sizing up, in a roomful of strangers, who can be trusted and who is likely to defect.

But even that is still, in a sense, selfishness in disguise. The following suggestion may not be.

I think uniquely in the animal kingdom, we humans make good use of the priceless gift of foresight. Contrary to popular misunderstandings, natural selection has no foresight. It couldn't have, for DNA is just a molecule and molecules can't think. If they could, they'd have seen the danger presented by contraception and nipped it in the bud long ago. But brains are another matter. Brains, if they are big enough, can run all sorts of hypothetical scenarios through their imaginations and calculate the consequences of alternative courses of action: "If I do such-and-such, I'll gain in the short term. But if I do so-and-so, although I'll have to wait for my reward, it'll be bigger when it comes." Ordinary evolution by natural selection, though an immensely powerful force for technical improvement, cannot look ahead in this way.

Our brains were endowed with the facility to set up goals and purposes. Originally, these goals would have been strictly in the service of gene survival: proximally the goal of killing a buffalo, the goal of finding a new water hole, the goal of kindling a fire, and so on. Still in the interests of gene survival, it was an advantage to make these goals as flexible as possible. New brain machinery, capable of deploying a hierarchy of re-programmable subgoals within goals, started to evolve.

Imaginative forethought of this kind was originally useful, but (in the genes'-eye view) it got out of hand. Brains as big as ours, as I've already argued, can actively rebel against the dictates of the naturally selected genes that built them. Using language, that other unique gift of the ballooning human brain, we can conspire together and devise political institutions, systems of law and justice, taxation, policing, public welfare, charity, and care for the disadvantaged. We can invent our own values. Natural selection gives rise to these only at second remove, by making brains that grow big. From the point of view of the selfish genes, our brains raced away with their emergent properties, and my personal value system regards this as a distinctly positive sign.

The Tyranny of the Texts

I have already disposed of one source of scepticism about this doctrine of rebellion against the selfish genes, in which radical, left-wing scientists wrongly smelled a concealed Cartesian dualism. A different kind of scepticism comes from religious sources. Time and again, religious critics have said to me something like this: "It is all very well issuing a call to arms against the tyranny of the selfish genes, but how do you decide what to put in its place? It's all very well sitting around a table with our big brains and our gift of foresight, but how are we going to agree on a set of values; how shall we decide what is good and what bad? What if somebody around the table advocates cannibalism as the answer to the world's protein shortage? What ultimate authority can we call up to dissuade them? Aren't we going to be sitting in an ethical vacuum where, in the absence of strong, textual authority, anything goes? Even if you don't believe the existence claims of religion, don't we need religion as a source of ultimate values?"

This is a genuinely difficult problem. I think we largely *are* in an ethical vacuum, and I mean all of us. If the hypothetical advocates of cannibalism were careful to specify road kills, who are already dead, they might even claim moral superiority over those who kill animals in order to eat them. There are still, of course, good counterarguments; for instance, the "distress to relatives" argument applies more strongly to humans than to other species; or there's the slippery slope argument ("If we get used to eating human road kills, it will be just a short step to . . ." and so on).[53]

So, I am not minimising the difficulties. But what I will now say is that we are no *worse* off than we were when we relied on ancient texts. The moral vacuum we now feel ourselves to be in has always been there, even if we haven't recognised it. Religious people are already entirely accustomed to picking and choosing *which* texts from holy books they obey and which they reject. There are passages of the Judaeo-Christian Bible which no modern Christian or Jew would wish to follow. The story of Isaac's narrowly averted sacrifice by his father Abraham strikes us moderns as a shocking piece of child abuse, whether we read it literally or symbolically.

Jehovah's appetite for burning flesh has no appeal for modern tastes. In Judges 11:31, Jephthah made a vow to God that, if God could guarantee Jephthah's victory over the children of Ammon, Jephthah would, without fail, sacrifice as a burnt offering "whatsoever cometh forth of the doors of my house to meet me, when I return." As luck would have it, this turned out to be Jephthah's own daughter, his only child. Understandably he rent his clothes, but there was nothing he could do about it, and his daughter very decently agreed that she should be sacrificed. She asked only that she should be allowed to go into the mountains for two months to bewail her virginity. At the end of this time, Jephthah slaughtered his own daughter and turned her into a burnt offering, as Abraham nearly had his son. God was not moved to intervene on this occasion.

Much of what we read of Jehovah makes it hard to see him as a good role model, whether we think of him as a factual or fictitious character. The texts show him to be jealous, vindictive, spiteful, capricious, humorless, and cruel. He was also, in modern terms, sexist, and an inciter to racial violence. When Joshua "utterly destroyed all that was in the city both man and woman, young and old, and ox, and sheep, and ass, with the edge of the sword," you might ask what the citizens of Jericho had done to deserve such a terrible fate. The answer is embarrassingly straightforward: they belonged to the wrong tribe. God had promised some Lebensraum to the children of Israel, and the indigenous population was in the way:

> But of the cities of these people, which the Lord thy God doth give thee for an inheritance, thou shalt save alive nothing that breatheth.
>   But thou shalt utterly destroy them; namely, the Hittites, and the Amorites, the Canaanites, and the Perrizzites, the Hivites, and the Jebusites; as the Lord thy God hath commanded thee.[54]

Now, of course, I'm being terribly unfair. The one thing a historian must never do is judge one era by the standards of a later era. But that is precisely my point. You cannot have it both ways. If you claim the right to pick and choose the nice bits of the Bible and sweep the nasty bits under the carpet, you have sold the pass. You have admitted that you do not, as a matter of fact, get your values from an ancient and authoritative holy book. You are demonstrably getting your values from some modern source, some contemporary liberal consensus or whatever it is. Otherwise, by what criterion do you choose the good bits of the Bible while rejecting, say, Deuteronomy's clear injunction to stone nonvirgin brides to death?

Wherever this contemporary liberal consensus may come from, I am entitled to appeal to it when I explicitly reject the authority of my ancient text—the DNA—just as you are entitled to appeal to it when you implicitly reject your—rather less ancient—texts from human scriptures. We can all sit down together and work out the values we want to follow. Whether we are talking about 4,000-year-old parchment scrolls, or 4,000-million-year-old DNA, we are all entitled to throw off the tyranny of the texts.

Notes

Amnesty Lecture, Sheldonian Theatre, Oxford, 30 January 1997. I thank Dr. Wes Williams and the other members of the organising committee for inviting me to give the lecture, Lalla Ward Dawkins for help in the preparation of it, and Dr. Williams for helpful editorial suggestions.

1. Quoted in Carl Sagan, *The Demon-Haunted World* (New York: Headline, 1996), p. 234. For a chilling collection and a justifiably savage indictment of drivel similar to that quoted here, including "cultural constructivism," "Afrocentric science," "feminist algebra," "science studies," and not forgetting Sandar Harding's "stirring assertion that Newton's *Principia Mathematica Philosophae Naturalis* is a 'rape manual,'" see Paul R. Gross and Norman Levitt, *Higher Superstition* (Baltimore: Johns Hopkins University Press, 1994), p. 131.

2. The "Dark Age" quotation is taken from Winston Churchill's speech delivered to the House of Commons, June 18, 1940, and later broadcast on the radio.

3. Daniel Bernoulli was the first to elaborate the principle according to which the pressure in a fluid decreases as its velocity increases.—*Ed.*

4. Sagan, *The Demon-Haunted World*, p. 33.

5. The following experience is commonplace. I recently was talking to a barrister, a young woman of high ideals specialising in criminal law defence. She expressed satisfaction that a private investigator whom she had employed had found evidence exonerating her client, who was accused of murder. I congratulated her and asked the obvious question: what would she have done if he had found evidence proving unequivocally that her client was guilty? Without hesitation, she said that she would quietly suppress the evidence. Let the prosecution find their own evidence. If they failed, more fool them. My outraged reaction to this story was one that she had obviously met many times when talking to non-lawyers, and I didn't blame her for wearily changing the subject rather than pursuing the argument.

6. E. O. Wilson, *Sociobiology* (Cambridge, Mass.: Harvard University Press, 1975), p. 28; R. Dawkins, *The Extended Phenotype* (Oxford: Oxford University Press, 1982), p. 1.

7. Examples are my own articles on astrology *(Independent on Sunday,* London, 31 December 1995, pp. 17–18) and on "paranormal" television *(Sunday Times,* London, 25 August 1996, sect. 3, p. 2). See also my Richard Dimbleby Lecture, "Science, Delusion and the Appetite for Wonder," originally broadcast on BBC Television and now visible on the World Wide Web at http://www.spacelab.net/~catalj/dimbleby.htm.

8. I recently heard of a London physicist who went to the lengths of refusing to pay his local government tax as long as the local adult education college advertised a course in astrology. An Australian professor of geology is in the process of suing a creationist for making money under false pretences by claiming to have found Noah's Ark. See commentary by Peter Pockley, *Daily Telegraph,* London, 23 April 1997.

9. M. White and J. Gribbin, *Einstein: A Life in Science* (London: Simon and Schuster, 1993).

10. Sagan, *The Demon-Haunted World*, p. 170.

11. Subrahmanyan Chandrasekhar, quoted in Martin Rees, *Before the Beginning* (London: Simon and Schuster, 1997), p. 103.

12. Carl Sagan, *Pale Blue Dot* (London: Headline, 1995), pp. 8–9.

13. This is a theme of my forthcoming book, *Unweaving the Rainbow,* to be published by Allen Lane in London and Houghton Mifflin in New York.

14. Charles Darwin, *The Origin of Species* (1859; reprint, London: The Folio Society, 1990), p. 287.

15. Iain Douglas-Hamilton and Oria Douglas-Hamilton, *Battle for the Elephants* (London: Doubleday, 1992), p. 220.

16. See Jonathan Glover's admirable *Causing Death and Saving Lives* (Harmondsworth: Penguin, 1977), a book so far-sighted that it was allowed to go out of print before scientific advances started to make it really topical.

17. R. Dawkins, "Gaps in the Mind," in P. Singer and P. Cavalieri, eds., *The Great Ape Project: Equality Beyond Humanity* (London: Fourth Estate, 1993), pp. 80–87.

18. Julian Huxley edited a compilation of his own and his grandfather's views on the subject. See T. H. and J. S. Huxley, *Touchstone for Ethics* (New York: Harper, 1947).

19. The first of his *Essays of a Biologist* (London: Chatto and Windus, 1926), entitled "Progress, Biological and Other," contained passages that read almost like a call to arms under evolution's banner: "[man's] face is set in the same direction as the main tide of evolving life, and his highest destiny, the end towards which he has so long perceived that he must strive, is to extend to new possibilities the process with which, for all these millions of years, nature has already been busy, to introduce less and less wasteful methods, to accelerate by means of his consciousness what in the past has been the work of blind unconscious forces" (p. 41).

20. See S. J. Gould, *Full House* (New York: Harmony Books, 1996) and my review of it, "Human Chauvinism," *Evolution* 51, no. 3 (1997), pp. 1015–1020.

21. T. H. Huxley, *Evolution and Ethics*, ed. J. Paradis and G. C. Williams (1894; reprint, Princeton: Princeton University Press, 1989).

22. The point has been made many times, from Darwin himself onwards. I devoted a chapter, "God's Utility Function," to it in *River Out of Eden* (London: Weidenfeld, 1994).

23. Richard Dawkins, "In Defence of Selfish Genes," *Philosophy* 56 (1981), pp. 556–573.

24. Steven Rose, "The Thatcher View of Human Nature," *New Scientist* 82 (17 May 1979), p. 575.

25. See the sociologist Ullica Segerstråle's penetrating analysis of this unsavoury episode: "Colleagues in Conflict: An 'In Vivo' Analysis of the Sociobiology Controversy," *Biology and Philosophy* 1 (1986), pp. 53–88. Also see Segerstråle, "Reductionism, 'Bad Science,' and Politics: A Critique of Anti-reductionist Reasoning," *Politics and the Life Sciences* 11, no. 2 (1986), pp. 199–214.

26. S. Rose, L. J. Kamin, and R. C. Lewontin, *Not in our Genes* (London: Penguin, 1984), p. 283. The order of authors, weirdly, is different from that in the American edition, in which Rose and Lewontin change places. My 1985 review of the book, in *New Scientist* 105, pp. 59–60, gives a full critique.

27. For a view of this topic which many scientists will find congenial, see Daniel C. Dennett, *Elbow Room: The Varieties of Free Will Worth Wanting* (Oxford: Oxford University Press, 1984).

28. H. G. Wells, *Anticipations of the Reaction of Mechanical and Scientific Progress upon Human Life and Thought* (London: Chapman and Hall, 1902) pp. 102–105.

29. Charles Darwin, *The Descent of Man* (New York: Appleton, 1871), vol. 2, p. 387.

30. Darwin, cited in H. Cronin, *The Ant and the Peacock* (Cambridge: Cambridge University Press, 1991), p. 352.

31. For a once-per-decade sampling of books on the subject, see Konrad Lorenz, *On Aggression* (New York: Harcourt, 1966); G. E. Pugh, *The Biological Origin of Human Values* (London: Routledge, 1977); R. D. Alexander, *The Biology of*

Moral Systems (New York: Aldine, 1987); M. Ridley, *The Origins of Virtue* (London: Viking, 1996).

32. J. Marchant, ed., *Alfred Russell Wallace: Letters and Reminiscences* (London: Cassell, 1916), vol. 1, p. 170.

33. A. R. Wallace, *Darwinism* (London: Macmillan, 1889).

34. J. Maynard Smith, "Optimisation Theory in Evolution," *Annual Review of Ecology and Systematics* 9 (1978), pp. 31–56.

35. N. K. Humphrey, "The Social Function of Intellect," in P. P. G. Bateson and R. A. Hinde, eds., *Growing Points in Ethology* (Cambridge: Cambridge University Press, 1976), pp. 303–317.

36. K. Lorenz, *Evolution and Modification of Behavior* (London: Methuen, 1966).

37. M. Konishi and F. Nottebohm, "Experimental Studies in the Ontogeny of Avian Vocalizations," in R. Hinde, ed., *Bird Vocalizations* (Cambridge: Cambridge University Press, 1969).

38. Marian Stamp Dawkins, the author of *Animal Suffering* (London: Chapman and Hall, 1980) and our leading investigator of the subject, has discussed with me the possibility that selective breeding of this sort might in theory provide a solution to some of the ethical problems of intensive animal husbandry. For instance, if present-day hens are unhappy in the confined conditions of battery cages, why not breed a race of hens that positively enjoy such conditions? She notes that people tend to greet such suggestions with repugnance (or humor, in the case of Douglas Adams's brilliant *The Restaurant at the End of the Universe*). Perhaps it conflicts with some deep-seated human value, perhaps some version of what has been called the "yuk factor." It is hard to see that it falls foul of dispassionate utilitarian reasoning, provided we could be sure the selective breeding genuinely changed the animal's perception of pain, rather than—horrifying thought—changing its method of responding to pain while leaving the perception of pain intact.

39. It is in this spirit that I named my own chapter on the subject "The Fortyfold Path to Enlightenment," *Climbing Mount Improbable* (London: Penguin, 1996).

40. For an elegant account, see S. Pinker, *The Language Instinct* (London: Viking, 1994).

41. The seminal volume on evolutionary psychology, with chapters by many of its leading practitioners, is J. H. Barkow, L. Cosmides, and J. Tooby, eds., *The Adapted Mind* (Oxford: Oxford University Press, 1992). Since this lecture was given, Steven Pinker's masterly *How the Mind Works* (London: Allen Lane, 1998) has appeared. If this brilliant book had been available before I gave this lecture, I would have said things differently.

42. J. Kingdon, *Self-made Man and His Undoing* (London: Simon and Schuster, 1993).

43. G. Orians and J. H. Heerwagen, "Evolved Responses to Landscapes," in J. H. Barkow, L. Cosmides, and J. Tooby, eds., *The Adapted Mind* (Oxford: Oxford University Press, 1992), pp. 555–579.

44. Orians and Heerwagen, "Evolved Responses to Landscapes," p. 569.

45. E. O. Wilson, *On Human Nature* (Cambridge, Mass.: Harvard University Press, 1978), p. 68. For a thorough treatment of fears and phobias by a psychologist taking a sympathetic view of evolutionary interpretations, see Isaac Marks, *Fears, Phobias, and Rituals* (Oxford: Oxford University Press, 1987).

46. Armen Alchian, quoted in Steven E. Landsburg, *The Armchair Economist* (London: Macmillan, 1993), p. 5.

47. I. Eibl-Eibesfeldt, *Human Ethology* (New York: Aldine de Gruyter, 1989).

48. N. A. Chagnon, "Mate Competition, Favoring Close Kin, and Village Fissioning Among the Yanomamö Indians," chap. 4 of N. A. Chagnon and W. Irons, eds., *Evolutionary Biology and Human Social Behaviour: An Anthropological Perspective* (Duxbury: North Scituate, Mass., 1979).

49. W. D. Hamilton, "Innate Social Aptitudes of Man: An Approach from Evolutionary Genetics," in *Narrow Roads of Gene Land: The Collected Papers of W. D. Hamilton* (New York and Oxford: W. H. Freeman, 1996), pp. 315–351.

50. R. Axelrod, *The Evolution of Cooperation* (New York: Basic Books, 1984; reprint, London: Penguin Books, 1990).

An earlier, pioneering treatment of the same theme is R. L. Trivers, "The Evolution of Reciprocal Altruism," *Quarterly Review of Biology* 46 (1971), pp. 35–57.

51. The general theory of such equilibrium calculations in evolution was worked out by John Maynard Smith. See his *Evolution and the Theory of Games* (Cambridge: Cambridge University Press, 1982).

52. M. Ridley, *The Origins of Virtue* (Harmondsworth: Penguin, 1996), p. 82.

53. It is for this reason that even I am a little shocked at the report (*The Independent on Sunday*, London, 18 January 1998) that a cookery show is to be broadcast on British television featuring (human) placenta pâté. The presenter of the show, a famous food writer, flash-fried strips of the placenta with shallots and blended two thirds into a purée. The rest was flambéed in brandy, and then sage and lime juice were added. The family of the baby concerned ate it, with twenty of their friends. The father thought it so delicious that he had fourteen helpings. It tasted, he thought, like a Mediterranean beef dish, and the mother (she is only twenty and this is her first child) declared that serving the placenta would become a family tradition. Now, eating the placenta is a common habit among mammals. It is doubtless nutritious, and natural selection may additionally favor it because of the danger of predators being attracted if the placenta is left lying around. There might seem to be no strictly logical argument against it. But still, I find the slippery slope argument persuasive. Placenta is human tissue, of the same genotype as the baby. The placenta is like an identical twin of the baby, which developed into a different form for a different purpose. If people come to realise this after the dish becomes a television-inspired restaurant delicacy, will this break what is probably the most powerful taboo in our consciousness? And do we really want to risk this, for the sake of a piece of culinary television frivolity? At the very least, the story sits oddly with the widespread antipathy against cloning human tissue for medical purposes.

54. Deuteronomy 20:16–17.

3

Science with Scruples

George Monbiot

I feel a little presumptuous talking about the ethics of science, as I am neither a scientist nor an ethicist. But over the last few years, new developments in the life sciences have begun to exert a profound impact on my particular interests: namely, the environment and social justice. What I want to talk about this evening is the scope of scientific enquiry itself, the applications of biological research in particular, and the ways in which they both affect existing environmental and social justice issues and establish new problems all of their own.

Following, as best we can, the daily developments in what we could call "the new biology"—new directions in molecular and, in particular, genetic research—it's hard to avoid the conclusion that this work could exert as profound an effect on human society as the splitting of the atom has done. In trying to shield ourselves from the ill effects of this new science while enjoying the benefits, I believe it would be a serious mistake to wait for the possible new biotechnologies to become either feasible or available before considering the ethical questions they raise. By then, I fear, technology will have taken the ethical decisions for us. New technologies emerge because, their developers hope, people will find them useful. If they are useful, there will be demand for them; if there is demand, society's ethics will change to accommodate them. The contraceptive pill is an obvious example.

But I would also argue that we should be looking not just at the technological applications of the new biology but also at the ethics of the science itself. Some people, notably Lewis Wolpert, chair of the Committee on the Public Understanding of Science, have argued that science is "value-free," that it carries, in other words, no ethical or moral implications. It is the simple search for information and the appeasement of scientific curiosity. It acquires ethical content only when the information it provides is applied. In what follows, I shall suggest that such an analysis cannot properly be said to provide an adequate account of new developments in biology.

In research institutes all over the country, potential commercial applications are held in view right at the inception of research programmes. In some cases, the same people pursue a line of enquiry all the way from hypothesis to marketplace. There is a simple reason for this. Many scientists are forced increasingly to rely on commercial funding or commercially oriented funding. The people who provide that funding have a somewhat less than dispassionate interest in the results of the research. Commercial funding and the forces that give rise to it are, of course, saturated with ethical implications. For these reasons, I believe that an attempt to divide research into pure science, which is value free, and applied science, which is value laden, is artificial in relation to the new biology.

It follows that there is a case for considering the ethical *implications* of the life sciences as a whole, rather than simply their possible *applications*. That being so, the first obvious question is, how have these sciences been changing over the last few years? The answer, to my ears, booms back loud and clear: there has been a narrowing of scientific horizons. We are at present faced with some of the most profound questions that humanity has ever confronted: vast environmental change, burgeoning global poverty, and dislocation and dispossession affecting billions of people. But just as these issues rear their heads, it seems to me that many scientists are turning away and refocusing on the submicroscopic. We are seeing in many faculties a movement away from some of the really critical areas—like primary health care, resource use, ecology, and conservation—and towards molecular biology and genetics.

Take forestry, for example. Now to my mind, and I think that some of you will share this perception, the great questions in forestry are, why are the forests disappearing? and what are the consequences of that disappearance? These are issues which involve tens of millions, or, according to the United Nations, hundreds of millions of people, affected by dispossession, soil erosion, hydrology, and local and possibly even regional climate change. We go to the forest scientists and ask them, why is this happening and what do we need to do to stop it? In reply, they give us gene sequences. We have seen molecular taxonomy taking over and pushing ecology out of some of the most prestigious forestry departments, just as we need sound ecological research more than ever before. It seems to me to be perverse, but it's not hard to see why it's happening.

For a start, molecular biology and genetics are very appealing, very exciting. You can't help feeling that you are standing on the edge of the known world and peering into the abyss of human ignorance. They are also, of course, easy to publish. Molecular biology presents a story with a beginning, a middle, and an end. It has a straightforward protocol, and the results are clear and decisive. A peer reviewer (the person who decides which papers are suitable for publication in academic journals) has no trouble concluding that the science is sound and the results are fit for dissemination. I would suggest that Sir Robert May's recent announcement that Britain is now the second-highest producer of scientific papers in the world might not be a great cause for celebration; what it might be reflecting is not the breadth of our science but the narrowness of it.

Now, your department's publication record is an important determinant of whether or not it is likely to get government funding: your eligibility is measured at least in part by the crude test of the number of papers you are producing. The nature of funding itself is, of course, changing, and this is also exerting a significant impact on the life sciences. In many branches of science, commercial funding is taking over from government funding. Even the allocation of government money (in the wake of the 1993 Government White Paper on Science and Technology) is guided increasingly by the possibility of commercial applications.

This introduces one simple problem: he who pays the piper calls the tune. The dispossessed of the world, the impoverished of the world, are the least likely to be able to pay, so they are the least likely to have their interests represented by the commercial funding of science. This means, in turn, that they are unlikely to be served by that science. It will pay less attention to their needs than to those, for example, of the big timber companies, which may be diametrically opposed to the interests of the poorest and most vulnerable people in the world. The genetic engineering of crop plants provides a clear example of some of the resultant dangers.

We are told, and many people believe, that the genetic engineering of farmed plants is going to feed the world, that indeed without it we have no prospect of feeding the world. There is no question that genetically engineered crops will, in many cases, produce higher yields than those that have not been genetically engineered. And there is also no question that, if it is not happening yet, we will soon get to the point at which, in absolute terms, we do not have enough food to feed the people of the world. A straightforward inference is evolved: we need more food and genetic engineering can provide more food, so genetic engineering will save the world from starvation.

Unfortunately, it is not as simple as that. Food crises all over the world, from the Irish potato famine to the disaster sweeping across northern Kenya today, result less from an absolute shortage of food than from the failure of food to find its way to the mouths of those who need it most. A major component of every famine in modern times has been the withdrawal of food from the needy and its accumulation by the sated—as it disappears abroad or is used for feeding intensively reared farm animals, or as essential staple crops are replaced by luxury foods. There are good reasons to suppose that the genetic engineering of crop plants is likely to contribute to this inequality and hence to famine.

For a couple of years at the beginning of the 1990s, I worked in Brazil. One of the issues I looked into was the connection between landowner-ship and food production. Some striking figures came to light. At the time, 1 percent of the landowners in Brazil owned 49 percent of the land, whereas the poorest 56 percent of landowners, the peasant farmers, owned between them just 3 percent of the land. And yet these people, farming just 3 percent of the land, produced nearly all the country's sta-ple crops: the majority of the manioc, maize, and beans that Brazil con-sumed and 40 percent of the rice. They were, in other words, feeding much of Brazil. The big landowners, by contrast, with plenty of capital and good international contacts, were using their estates to produce cash crops for export.[1]

I found this very interesting, and so I started asking the same questions in other countries. A pattern began to emerge: those who had the money and the international contacts used these advantages to make much big-ger profits than they would earn by growing rice or beans for local peo-ple. They might be growing pineapples, tea, flowers for sale abroad, or cereals on a vast scale to sell to Europe for pig feed. It became clear to me that anything that helps small farmers encourages food security, whereas anything that tramples on small farmers reduces the possibility of food security.

Now, the genetic engineering of crop plants relies on what could be de-scribed as one-sided intellectual property rights. To ensure that they reap the benefits of their investments, the corporations that produce them are applying for, and obtaining, patents on genetically engineered crop plants. Many of the plants that the big pharmaceutical companies use as their raw material have been developed over hundreds or even thou-sands of years by peasant cultivators. The corporations take them to their laboratories, play around with them for eighteen months, stick in a floun-der gene here and a llama gene there, and hope to produce a lucrative new product. It might have a longer growing season, for example, resis-tance to frost or to pests, or a better response to fertilizer.

Those crops are expensive, and many of them are made more expen-sive still because they have been engineered to respond to chemicals which the same companies just happen to produce. But what makes them particularly inaccessible to the small farmers is that they can't do what they used to do, which is to buy seed just once, thereafter growing and saving seed of their own. Having patented these new germ lines, the big companies are insisting that every time a farmer grows seed for the following year, the corporation should receive a royalty. Small farmers, many of whom work outside the cash economy, simply cannot compete on these terms. As big producers gain access to technologies beyond the reach of the poor, they will secure an even more powerful grip on land tenure and production; we will see an exacerbation of the inequalities inherent in the technology-driven boost to food production in the Third World known as the Green Revolution. It is my contention that this will result in a reduction of food security worldwide.

This inequality is not the only problem raised by the genetic engineering of crop plants. When they first began to look like a major future component of agricultural production, five or six years ago, we were promised two things. The first was that they would enable us to reduce our dependence on pesticides. We would no longer have to inflict these toxins on the environment because plants would be equipped to cope with their pests by themselves: new genetic material would make them unpalatable or even poisonous to their predators. They would also be able to out-compete the weeds that might grow alongside them in the field. We were promised that the new crops would extend consumer choice: we would always be able to choose whether or not we wished to consume genetically engineered products. But no sooner did the first major shipment of genetically engineered crop plants arrive than both of these promises were thrown straight out of the window.

Last year the United States started attempting to export large quantities of genetically engineered "Roundup Ready" soybeans produced by the pharmaceutical company Monsanto. Now Roundup, or glyphosate, is a herbicide also produced by Monsanto, which, as its name suggests, was developed to kill any plant, of any species, it comes into contact with. The "Roundup Ready" soybean is the one thing that isn't destroyed by glyphosate. It means that soya farmers are released from the complicated business of applying selective herbicides: you can destroy everything in the field that's not a soya plant with one deadly weapon. The likely result, of course, is fields with even less biodiversity than survives at the moment.

Moreover, when the United States was proposing to start exporting these genetically engineered soybeans to Britain, it argued that it would be very difficult to keep them apart from ordinary soybeans and wanted to mix the whole lot in together. Over the last two years Monsanto has spent $2 billion in acquiring seed breeding and supply companies in the United States—it will soon become hard not to buy Monsanto products. Soya derivatives are found in between 50 and 60 percent of all the processed foods consumed in the United Kingdom. The mixing of genetically engineered soybeans with ordinary ones means that consumers eating processed food will have no choice as to whether or not they eat the products of genetic engineering.

There is, however, one agricultural application of genetic engineering that does have the potential to reduce pesticide use, and that is the production of genetically modified organisms designed to attack crop pests. It sounds like a good idea—viruses could, in theory, be specifically programmed to kill a single pest species, leaving the rest of the ecosystem intact. In Oxford a couple of years ago, we were lucky enough to witness the first launch of genetically modified organisms into the British environment, courtesy of the Institute of Virology. The institute proposed to release a genetically engineered virus designed to attack a species of caterpillar that would be eating some experimental cabbages just outside Wytham Woods, 3 or 4 miles from Oxford. The Natural Environmental Research Council, which provides much of the institute's money, insisted that it publicise the proposed trials and hold a public meeting at which ordinary people could find out more about the project and raise any concerns they might have.

The Institute of Virology conformed to these instructions to the letter. A tiny advert appeared in the classified section of the local paper, giving notice of the public meeting. Fortunately, a resident of Wytham village was glancing through the small ads and stumbled across it. He told his friends what he had found, who in turn got hold of some academics and environmentalists in Oxford, myself among them, hoping to find out more. No one knew anything, so we got in touch with the institute and applied for tickets to the meeting.

We were told it was sold out. We found this a little odd, as the advert had only just been published, and it wasn't exactly eye-catching. So we asked a friend of ours in London, with good scientific credentials and who was known to the institute, to apply. She was sent a ticket right away. We called the institute and asked what was happening. Tickets, they told us, were to be handed out only to people selected by the director.

Now, to my mind there was an evident public need to know what was going on, how the experiment was going to be run, and what, if any, dangers it posed to the ecosystem. We turned up at the meeting, but they wouldn't let us in. So we got into our sleeping bags, put on red noses and antennae and, as giant human caterpillars, clambered over the roofs of the institute.

It worked. We succeeded in luring out representatives of the institute to explain to us what was going on. There were, we came to see, several causes for continued alarm. The field trials, for example, had not been preceded by experiments in a "biological greenhouse," in which field conditions are simulated to see whether or not there was any danger of the virus escaping. The virus had not been genetically disabled. Nor was it as specific to the host caterpillar as the institute had suggested. It turned out that forty-three butterfly and moth species were known to be susceptible to the virus, with the possibility that other organisms could also be affected. We discovered that the means of containing the virus and preventing it from leaving the cabbage patch consisted of a coarse plastic mesh. We further discovered that the leading virologist on the Advisory Committee on Releases into the Environment, which licensed the experiment, was also a member of staff at the Institute of Virology.

There can scarcely be a clearer illustration of the need for transparency and accountability at all stages of research and development. For, clearly, one of the casualties of the transgression of the protocols of science is the distinction between the practical application and ethical implications of research. When the public is kept in the dark, it is bad not only for democracy but also, in the long run, for science, which loses credibility and public confidence.

Unfortunately, especially when their work is commercially funded, faculties seem, if anything, to be tightening their grip on information about what they are doing. One of the principal reasons why is the patentability of both genetic material and the processes required to manipulate that material. If you are hoping to monopolise the fruits of your labor, the last thing you want to do is to disclose your evidence before you file your patent application. In other words we, the public, are becoming less and less likely to hear about what science is doing until that science is turned into technology and it's too late to ask the critical ethical questions.

Patent law also raises its own problems. In 1995 the European Commission, for the first time ever, had a draft directive rejected by the European Parliament. The directive was attempting to expand the range of biological "inventions" that could be patented. European parliamentarians, particularly the German members of the European Parliament (MEPs), were concerned that it was so loosely drafted as more or less to confer patentability on life itself. In response, the European Commission has now produced a new draft directive. Far from solving the problem, it seems merely to have made the situation even more confused.

According to the draft directive, you can now file and receive a patent on genetic manipulations of plants and animals in general but not on what it calls plant and animal "varieties." Confused? So was I, so I went to see one of Britain's top patent lawyers, a man called Kevin Mooney at Simmonds and Simmonds in the City of London. I showed him the directive and asked him what it meant. After reading it three times, he told me he hadn't the faintest idea. As far as he and I could work out, what it seemed to be saying is that you can apply for a patent for a genetic modification of all tomatoes or even of all plants, but you can't apply for a patent on a genetic modification of a particular breed of tomato. It seems that American patent law has been interpreted in the same way. W. R. Grace, a big pharmaceutical company, has received a patent for all genetic modifications of all cotton.[2]

The ethics of ownership are surely never more pressing than when applied to human genetic material. But here again, the European draft directive has fudged the issue. It says that you cannot apply for a patent on human genetic material inside the body, but you can get a patent on precisely the same chemicals extracted from the body and purified. But of course, this is no real barrier to patenting at all, and the law here provides no protection. Except, that is, to those who wish to use genetic material commercially, for it only becomes commercially valuable when it has been extracted and purified. The sloppy drafting of patent law is already beginning to precipitate some surreal and, I feel, outrageous situations. I recently visited a very eminent geneticist at the company Smith Kline Beecham and, in passing, asked him if he had any patents of his own. He thought for a moment and then suddenly remembered. "Ah yes," he said, "I own the gene for human maleness."

Developments in science are bringing about a drastic realignment of property relations. Things that once belonged to the commonweal or weren't even perceived as belonging to anyone or anything at all are suddenly being claimed as private property. I find this deeply worrying and nowhere more so than when mediated by something called the Human Genome Diversity Project.

The Human Genome Diversity Project is a multinational project whose purpose is to prospect for unusual and interesting genes around the world. Its proponents claim that they want to preserve the germ lines of indigenous people before they become extinct, so that their genes will continue to be useful for potential medical or commercial applications after they've gone.

As you might have guessed, there was not a great deal of consultation with indigenous people before this project began. Had there been, the researchers would have heard that indigenous people aren't very interested in having their genomes preserved after they've become extinct but are far more interested in not becoming extinct in the first place. Human beings are not, they would have pointed out, crop varieties, to be stored and selected for other people's use. Neither should they be perceived as divisible sources of commodities. If indigenous people want any help from the outside world, they want help in creating the social and economic conditions that would give them a better chance of survival, not in deciding how to use their remains after they've gone.

But consultation is not one of this programme's notable features. Indeed, for all the protestations of its adherents, you can't help beginning to suspect that it might be guided by motives even less elevated than those they have claimed for it. Researchers funded by the Human Genome Diversity Project have been working amongst the Hagahai people of New Guinea. They came across a gene sequence that was of particular interest to them. It seems to confer resistance to a rare form of leukaemia. Their samples were handed over to the National Institutes of Health in Washington, which applied for and received a patent on the leukaemia-resisting sequence. This institute in Washington, in other words, secured rights over part of the Hagahai people that could, in law, be used to fend off a Hagahai claim that that part in fact belongs to them. Without their consent or even an effective attempt to inform them about what was going on, ownership of what could be described as the essence of those people had been transferred.[3]

Although the ethical implications of the Human Genome Diversity Project may be pretty mind blowing, the implications of the Human Genome Project are, if anything, further reaching. The Human Genome Project is also a multilateral programme. It is huge and well-funded, and its protagonists hope that it will produce a complete map of the human genome within the next five or ten years. Some of the potential applications are tremendously exciting.

For example, gene mapping could lead to much more precise medical diagnoses. It's possible that in a few years' time, genetic testing could become as routine as blood testing is today. A doctor could take a genetic sample, send it to the lab, and a week or two later see exactly which genetic deficiency you might be suffering from. A more precise diagnosis can, of course, lead to a more precise cure.

It sounds great, but some of the implications are alarming. The first is the possibility that other people get hold of information about our genetic makeup. It's a particularly pertinent worry in Britain, where we currently have no privacy rights. In the United States, where health care largely depends on health insurance, insurers are already practising what could only be described as genetic discrimination. Already there are numerous cases of companies writing people off as a bad bet because a relative of theirs has a genetic disease, and this is done in the absence of firm genetic information. One can envisage a situation in which, with much better access to information and a much more empirical basis for deciding who should be regarded as "genetically defective," there is a wholesale withdrawal of insurance from big sections of the population. Insurance would cease to be risky for the insurers and cease to be useful to those who might need it most.

The situation looks still worse when it comes to employment and education. Again this issue is, at the moment, most urgent in the United States. There have been several cases, documented by Lisa Geller of Harvard Medical School, of employers sacking people on the grounds that they have a genetic predisposition to disease. Their companies don't want to spend money training people who are likely to drop dead at forty. But gene mapping has a more controversial application than straightforward medical diagnosis. Already, unborn foetuses can be screened for certain genetic defects that would ensure, if they are born, that they suffer a brief and horrible life. Embryos carrying these mutations could be aborted. The big question this raises, of course, is "Where should the line be drawn?" Should this screening be applied to the whole genome and allowed to extend to conditions that aren't so immediately life threatening? In this case, we're not talking about some hazy future, but about issues which already need urgently to be resolved. Hammersmith Hospital in London has been one of the pioneers of in vitro fertilisation. To ensure that it is not putting time and resources into producing foetuses with serious defects, it has been screening embryos' genomes for certain conditions. At the end of 1995, the hospital was producing embryos for a couple whose family history suggested a hereditary predisposition towards a certain kind of bowel cancer, which does not normally strike until people are in their thirties or forties. They wanted their embryos screened for that cancer. It caused a major controversy, as people perceived that the line was already beginning to get blurred.

When we're not certain about where the boundary ought to lie between acceptable and unacceptable genetic screening, we are in danger of stepping into some very dangerous territory indeed. If it's acceptable to screen out embryos whose conditions are likely to be immediately life threatening, why is it not also acceptable to screen out embryos whose conditions might be life threatening later on? And if that is acceptable, why is it not reasonable to screen out embryos whose conditions will make their lives uncomfortable? And if that is okay, why should we not screen out embryos which might be at a disadvantage by comparison to other people—who might be short, ugly, or unintelligent, for example? I find it hard to present a coherent argument for drawing the line in one place rather than another. It certainly presents the liberals among us with something of an ethical problem. We recoil from the idea of selecting one human being while rejecting others, especially on the grounds of, say, parental vanity or ambition. Yet we support a woman's right to terminate her pregnancy, even if it's for no better reason than that it would interfere with her career or a hitherto carefree life.

The issue becomes still more fraught with the possibility that germline gene therapy might one day become a viable means of changing the genetic characteristics of an embryo. Germline gene therapy—attempting to clip bits of genetic material into or out of an embryonic human genome—is wisely not permitted in this country, and neither is it feasible at the moment. But we would be wrong to suppose that, were it ever to become possible, it would necessarily be unpopular. Theresa Marteau, a health psychologist at St Thomas's and Guy's Hospital in London, documented what might be the start of a rapid rise in public acceptability for this putative technology. She performed two surveys, one in 1993 and one in 1994. In 1993, 4 percent of respondents said they would be in favor of gene therapy for their own embryos, to enhance their intelligence or appearance or to ensure that they did not turn out to be homosexuals. By 1994, the figure had risen to 11 percent.

We've already heard the outcry over the decision by the Human Fertilisation and Embryology Authority not to allow Diane Blood to attempt to use the genetic material of her dead husband—his sperm—in order to conceive a child. When these technologies become available, when there are quick fixes for hitherto insoluble human problems and tragedies, people will demand that they be made available. Were germline gene therapy to become legal for life-saving purposes, it is possible to conceive of a similar public outcry in the future resulting from a decision to withhold it from people wishing to enhance the characteristics of their children. So, given that continuing to block the development of this technology might be unpopular, would it also be wrong? Some people have argued that there's really no difference between choosing your children's genes and choosing to have them educated privately. One of the reasons why I find the new genetics so terrifying is that I think they might be right.

Assuming—as I think we can—that the new technologies are likely only to be available to a small number of people on the basis of their ability to pay, then, like private schools, they will confer an advantage on some people at the expense of others, irrespective of merit. Just as the escape hatch of the public school enables the wealthiest and most influential people in the country to ignore the underfunding of state education, future genetic screening or gene therapy could allow them to buy their way out of concern for the social and environmental factors that contribute to poor health. Indeed, it's not hard to imagine a future in which only the rich could—through gene technology—escape from the genetic effects of increasing exposure to such pollutants as pesticide residues and radioactive waste. The prospective gene technologies have the capacity to petrify, even more effectively than private schools, society's heritable inequity.

But there might also be more immediate effects. The moment at which something looks like it can be "fixed" is the moment at which it becomes widely perceived as "broken": the possibility of eliminating purportedly gay foetuses will surely contribute to the public disparagement of homosexuality. It is also possible to picture a world in which those whose genomes have been selected or enhanced could feel themselves set apart from those who have not been manipulated. With some justification, the genetic elect could claim that they did not share a common humanity with the genetically unscreened, and the racism, sexism, and classism we suffer from today would find a new and potentially even more virulent outlet.

What's good for the individual, in other words, may be bad for society. As I see it, the dangers with which the possibility of germline gene therapy confronts us emerge not—as some people have suggested—from the threat of a coercive state seeking racial improvement but from the less fashionable bogey of mass consumerism.

This possibility brings us back to the central point of this talk: that technology governs ethics if ethics do not first govern technology. This, of course, is exactly what we have seen with the development of the motorcar, another case in which what is good for the individual might not be good for society. Long ago, men with red flags had to walk in front of motorcars. In view of the horrendous toll of deaths and injuries inflicted by cars since the lifting of that prescription, it begins to look as if the man with the red flag was quite a sensible idea. Once the technology became more widely available and more powerful, however, and the man in front of the car began to look more absurd, the urge to go faster, to enjoy the convenience and excitement of speed swiftly overrode concerns for other people's safety. The car, at first an idle luxury, became an irremovable feature of human society, which had to change its values enormously to accommodate it. If we don't want to be doomed to succumb to the same bizarre valuation in the future—putting convenience ahead of human life—then we must start introducing an ethical framework early enough to forestall the introduction of disastrous new technology. But how do we do it without also eliminating some of the great benefits the new biology can confer?

I would like to suggest that in some branches of this science the answer is quite easy to come by. There are some developments that, with a certain degree of confidence, I think we can say are simply wrong. The Human Genome Diversity Project, for example, is a diabolical scheme and should be stopped dead. Information about our genetic makeup should be governed by the strictest possible privacy legislation. Consumers should be able to choose whether or not they eat genetically engineered products. The intellectual property rights of small farmers should be upheld, and genetic material, which is, of course, by no stretch of the imagination a human "invention," should surely not be possible to patent.

Thereafter, however, it all gets a lot more complicated. The lines we'll have to draw if we are, collectively, to defend the public interest may not be obvious ones. There are unlikely to be clear and ethically consistent means of deciding where they lie. They will leave some people feeling aggrieved and resentful. This means we must be very careful to consult as widely as possible, rather than handing down judgements from on high, as has been perceived to be the case with certain ethical decisions about scientific developments in the past. This process could only work if it's accompanied by a massive exercise in public information, showing people not only what is happening and what the promises of this new biology are but what the dangers are as well. Breathless reporting of "miracle cures" must be balanced with words of warning about the possible adverse consequences. It is, I believe, a mistake to assume that people are not capable of understanding this new science and its consequences. If you treat people like intelligent sentient beings, they will respond as such. If 1 million peasant farmers, most of them illiterate, can take to the streets of Bangalore in southern India in protest at the implications of trade-related intellectual property rights as negotiated in the Uruguay Round of the General Agreement on Tariffs and Trade, I don't see why people in this country can't get involved in debates about biotechnology.

Having made the decisions about what we don't want, how do we make them stick? How do we prevent the ethical barrier we have erected in front of, for example, germline gene therapy being swept aside like the man with the red flag? I don't think it would be either desirable or practical to ban certain lines of scientific inquiry. But nor should it be necessary. Now that so much research is tied, from its inception onward, to its possible technological applications, banning a particular technology will, in practice, amount to terminating the research that might lead to that technology. When companies see that there's no prospect of making money, the necessary research won't be funded, and the fruits of the tree of knowledge will not end up dangling temptingly in front of us.

This does not mean, of course, that a technological ban we impose today will last forever. The best we can hope for is to establish an ethical framework now, which at the very least can help future generations to establish their own ethical frameworks in the absence of urgent commercial pressures. The alternative is simply to let the market have its head and wholly subordinate the interests of society to the interests of the individual.

There's a clear role for both ethicists and lawmakers in seeking to establish boundaries for the new biology, but what about the scientists themselves? It is surely time for them too to start exercising their ethical judgement, and they could start from the position that science is not value free. Researchers do not inhabit a planet of their own but remain part of society, which exercises a powerful influence over which topics they investigate and where their investigations can lead them. As members of that society and as the brains behind the research and its technological applications, scientists must accept that their work carries a burden of responsibility.

Sometimes this can mean being faced with some very hard choices indeed. In 1996, Edinburgh University's Centre for Human Ecology was working on precisely the sort of big questions whose answers are going to be critical to the future welfare of vast numbers of people: the political factors leading to environmental destruction and the links between social exclusion and resource depletion. The university didn't like this at all, principally, it seems, because some of its funders were very uncomfortable with the centre's findings. Within the same fortnight that it decided that Christopher Brand, the so-called scientific racist, should stay on, the university shut down the Centre for Human Ecology.

The researchers there, some of whom were eminent and highly employable, could have done what many others would have done, seeking uncontentious work in other faculties or other universities. But they stuck to their guns. They saw that nowhere else would let them function as an effective unit, working on the issues they knew to be important. They kept the centre together and set it up in a farmhouse 30 miles from Edinburgh. The Centre for Human Ecology is now a desperately underfunded, independent organisation, whose members rely on social security, donations, and voluntary work from concerned scientists around the world. They have done the right thing, and it hurts. I am afraid that this is the sort of choice that many scientists who are prepared to shoulder their responsibilities might have to face. They will not get big money to answer big questions. The big money is reserved for the small questions, whereas the big ones attract only tiny amounts of funding.

It's time that we started to concentrate on asking and trying to answer the big questions, however painful it might be. The world is best apprehended with the naked eye, not the gene sequencing machine.

Notes

1. For more on this, see G. Monbiot, *Amazon Watershed* (London: Michael Joseph, 1991).—*Ed.*

2. For more on the question of genetic patenting in general and the particular points raised here, see *The Ecologist* 26, no. 5 (September-October 1996).

3. This has recently been successfully contested. For more on this, see the work done by the Genetics Forum and the Rural Advancement Foundation International; their addresses, along with those of other interest groups and sources of information, are given in notes at the conclusion of this lecture.

A Note to the Reader

What follows are addresses and Websites where readers can find further information about the issues raised here.

Food Bytes. News and analysis on genetic engineering and factory farming by
Ronnie Cummins, Pure Food Campaign USA
e-mail: alliance@mr.net
Website: http://www.geocities.com/Athens/1527

Friends of the Earth. 26–28 Underwood Street
London, N1 7JQ
United Kingdom
Website: http://www.foe.co.uk

Gaia Foundation. 18 Well Walk
London NW3 1LD
United Kingdom

Genetics Forum
94 White Lion Street, 2nd floor
London N1 9PF
United Kingdom
E-mail: geneticsforum@gn.apc.org

Publishes *The Splice of Life* magazine (ISSN 1362–1955)
Genetix Update
P.O. Box 9656
London N4 4JY
United Kingdom
Website: http://home.rednet.co.uk/homepages/davestee/gen.html

Pesticide Action Network. North America Updates Service
E-mail: panna@panna.org
Website: http://www.panna.org/panna

Further Useful Websites

Corporate watch
Website: http://www.corpwatch.org/home.html

Euro/British legislation
Website: http://biosafety.ihe.be/GB/Leg_EurGB.html

European Parliament news releases
Website: http://www.epa.gov/opptintr/biotech/biorule.htm

GLOBAL 2000
Austrian campaign site, in German
Website: http://www.t0.or.at/~global2000/gentech.html

Greenpeace bio-tech information and campaign highlights
Website: http://www.greenpeace.org/~comms/cbio/geneng.html

Greenpeace NLP pure food campaign
Website: http://www.netlink.de/gen/info.html

Information on food defamation laws in the United States:
Website: http://web.its.smu.edu/~dmcnickl/miscell/pfcamp.html

Monsanto's homepage
Website: http://www.monsanto.com/

Reuters health information
Website: http://www.reutershealth.com

Swedish site on intellectual property rights
Institute for Agriculture and Trade Policy
Website: http://www.netlink.de/gen/biopiracy.html

Supreme Court Index
Website: http://lcs.usatoday.com/news/court/nscot000.htm

"Super heroes against genetics"
Website: http://www.envirolink.org/orgs/shag/genetix.html

Rural Advancement Foundation International (RAFI)
Campaigns against unfair patenting and bio-piracy
Website: http://www.rafi.ca/misc/courting.html

4

What Shall We Tell the Children?

Nicholas Humphrey

"Sticks and stones may break my bones, but words will never hurt me," the proverb goes. And since, like most proverbs, this one captures at least part of the truth, it makes sense that Amnesty International should have devoted most of its efforts to protecting people from the menace of sticks and stones, not words. Worrying about words must have seemed something of a luxury.

Still the proverb, like most proverbs, is also in part obviously false. The fact is that words *can* hurt. For a start, they can hurt people indirectly by inciting others to hurt them: a crusade preached by a pope, racist propaganda from the Nazis, malevolent gossip from a rival. They can hurt people not so indirectly by inciting them to take actions that harm themselves: the lies of a false prophet, the blackmail of a bully, the flattery of a seducer. And words can hurt directly, too: the lash of a malicious tongue, the dreaded message carried by a telegram, the spiteful onslaught that makes the hearer beg the tormentor say no more.

Sometimes, indeed, mere words can kill outright. There is a story by Christopher Cherniak about a deadly "word-virus" that appeared one night on a computer screen.[1] It took the form of a brain-teaser, a riddle so paradoxical that it fatally twisted the mind of all those who heard or read it, making that person fall into an irreversible coma. A fiction? Yes, of course. But a fiction with some horrible parallels in the real world. There have been all too many examples historically of how words can take possession of a person's mind, destroying the will to live. Think, for example, of so-called voodoo death. The witch-doctor has merely to cast a spell of death on someone, and within hours the victim will collapse and die. Or, on a larger and more dreadful scale, think of the mass suicide at Jonestown in Guyana in 1972. The cult leader Jim Jones had only to plant certain crazed ideas in the heads of his disciples, and at his signal, nine hundred of them willingly drank cyanide.

"Words will never hurt me"? The truth may rather be that words have a unique power to hurt. And if we were to make an inventory of the man-made causes of human misery, it would be words, not sticks and stones, that head the list. Even guns and high explosives might be considered playthings by comparison. As Vladimir Mayakovsky wrote in his poem "I": "On the pavement / of my trampled soul / the soles of madmen / stamp the print of rude, crude, words."[2]

Should we then be fighting Amnesty's battle on this front too? Should we be campaigning for the rights of human beings to be protected from verbal oppression and manipulation? Do we need "word laws," just as all civilised societies have gun laws, licensing who should be allowed to use them in what circumstances? Should there be Geneva protocols es-tablishing what kinds of speech count as crimes against humanity?

No. The answer, I'm sure, ought in general to be, "No, don't even think of it." Freedom of speech is too precious a freedom to be meddled with. And however painful some of its consequences may sometimes be for some people, we should still as a matter of principle resist putting curbs on it. By all means, we should try to make up for the harm that other peo-ple's words do, but not by censoring the words as such.

Since I am so sure of this in general, and since I'd expect most of you to be so, too, I shall probably shock you when I say it is the purpose of my lecture today to argue in one particular area just the opposite. To argue, in short, in favor of censorship, against freedom of expression, and to do so moreover in an area of life that has traditionally been regarded as sacrosanct.

I am talking about moral and religious education, and especially the ed-ucation a child receives at home, where parents are allowed—even ex-pected—to determine for their children what counts as truth and false-hood, right and wrong. Children, I'll argue, have a human right not to have their minds crippled by exposure to other people's bad ideas—no matter *who* these other people are. Parents, correspondingly, have no god-given licence to enculturate their children in whatever ways they person-ally choose: no right to limit the horizons of their children's knowledge, to bring them up in an atmosphere of dogma and superstition, or to insist they follow the straight and narrow paths of their own faith.

In short, children have a right not to have their minds addled by non-sense, and we as a society have a duty to protect them from it. So we should no more allow parents to teach their children to believe, for exam-ple, in the literal truth of the Bible or that the planets rule their lives, than we should allow parents to knock their children's teeth out or lock them in a dungeon.

That's the negative side of what I want to say. But there will be a positive side as well. If children have a right to be protected from false ideas, they have, too, a right to be succoured by the truth. And we as a society have a duty to provide it. Therefore, we should feel as much obliged to pass on to our children the best scientific and philosophical understanding of the natural world—to teach, for example, the truths of evolution and cosmology or the methods of rational analysis—as we already feel obliged to feed and shelter them.

I don't suppose you'll doubt my good intentions here. Even so, I realise there may be many in this audience—especially the more liberal of you—who do not like the sound of this at all: neither the negative, nor still less the positive side of it. In which case, among the good questions you may have for me, will probably be these.

First, what is all this about "truths" and "lies"? How could anyone these days have the face to argue that the modern scientific view of the world is the only *true* view that there is? Haven't the postmodernists and relativists taught us that more or less anything can be true in its own way? What possible justification could there be, then, for presuming to protect children from one set of ideas or to steer them towards another, if in the end all are equally valid?

Second, even supposing that in some boring sense the scientific view really is "more true" than some others, who's to say that this truer worldview is the *better* one? At any rate, the better for everybody? Isn't it possible—or actually likely—that particular individuals, given who they are and what their life situation is, would be better served by one of the not-so-true worldviews? How could it possibly be right to insist on teaching children to think this modern way when, in practice, the more traditional way of thinking might actually work best for them?

Third, even in the unlikely event that almost everybody really would be happier and better off if they were brought up with the modern scientific picture, do we—as a global community—really want everyone right across the world thinking the same way, everyone living in a dreary scientific monoculture? Don't we want pluralism and cultural diversity—a hundred flowers blooming, a hundred schools of thought contending?

And then, last, why—when it comes to it—should *children's* rights be considered so much more important than those of other people? Everyone would grant, of course, that children are relatively innocent and relatively vulnerable, and so may have more need of protection than their seniors do. Still, why should their special rights in this respect take precedence over everybody else's rights in other respects? Don't parents have their own rights too, their rights *as* parents? The right, most obviously, to be parents, or literally to bring forth and *prepare* their children for the future as *they* see fit?

Good questions? Knock-down questions, some of you may think, and questions to which any broad-minded and progressive person could give only one answer. I agree they are good-ish questions and ones that I should deal with. But I don't think it is by any means so obvious what the answers are, especially for a liberal. Indeed, were we to change the context not so greatly, most people's liberal instincts would, I'm sure, pull quite the other way.

Let's suppose we were talking not about children's minds but children's bodies. Suppose the issue were not who should control a child's intellectual development but who should control the development of her hands or feet . . . or genitalia. Let's suppose, indeed, that this is a lecture about female circumcision. And the issue is not whether anyone should be permitted to deny a girl knowledge of Darwin but whether anyone should be permitted to deny her the uses of a clitoris.

And now here I am suggesting that it is a girl's right to be left intact, that parents have no right to mutilate their daughters to suit their own sociosexual agenda, and that we as a society ought to prevent it. What's more, I want to make the positive case as well, that every girl should actually be encouraged to find out how best to use to her own advantage the intact body she was born with. Would you still have those good questions for me? And would it still be so obvious what the liberal answers are? There will be a lesson—even if an awful one—in hearing how the questions sound.

First, what's all this about "intactness" and "mutilation"? Haven't the anthropological relativists taught us that the idea of there being any such thing as "absolute intactness" is an illusion and that girls are—in a way—just as intact without their clitorises?

Anyway, even if uncircumcised girls are in some boring sense "more intact," who's to say that intactness is a virtue? Isn't it possible that some girls, given their life situation, would actually be better off being not so intact? What if the men of their culture consider intact women unmarriageable?

Besides, who wants to live in a world where all women have standard genitalia? Isn't it essential to maintaining the rich tapestry of human culture that there should be at least a few groups where circumcision is still practised? Doesn't it indirectly enrich the lives of all of us to know that some women somewhere have had their clitorises removed?

In any case, why should it be only the rights of the girls that concern us? Don't other people have rights in relation to circumcision also? How about the rights of the circumcisers themselves, their rights *as* circumcisers? Or the rights of mothers to do what they think best, just as in their day was done to them?

You'll agree, I hope, that the answers go the other way now. But maybe some of you are going to say that this is not playing fair. Whatever the superficial similarities between doing things to a child's body and doing things to her mind, there are also several obvious and important differences. For one thing, the effects of circumcision are final and irreversible, whereas the effects of even the most restrictive regime of education can perhaps be undone later. For another, circumcision involves the removal of something that is already part of the body and will naturally be missed, whereas education involves selectively adding new things to the mind that would otherwise never have been there. To be deprived of the pleasures of bodily sensation is an insult on the most personal of levels, but to be deprived of a way of thinking is perhaps no great personal loss.

So, you might argue, the analogy is far too crude for us to learn from it. And those original questions about the rights to control a child's education still need addressing and answering on their own terms.

Very well. I'll try to answer them just so—and we shall see whether or not the analogy with circumcision was unfair. But there may be another kind of objection to my project that I should deal with first. For it might be argued, I suppose, that the whole issue of intellectual rights is not worth bothering with, since so few of the world's children are in point of fact at risk of being hurt by any *severely* misleading forms of education— and those who are, are mostly far away and out of reach.

Now that I say it, however, I wonder whether anyone could make such a claim with a straight face. Look around—close to home. We ourselves live in a society where most adults—not just a few crazies, but most adults—subscribe to a whole variety of weird and nonsensical beliefs that in one way or another they shamelessly impose upon their children.

In the United States, for example—which I take as the example since it's where I currently reside—it sometimes seems that almost everyone is either a religious fundamentalist or a New Age mystic or both. And even those who aren't will scarcely dare admit it. Opinion polls confirm that, for example, a full 98 percent of the U.S. population say they believe in God, 70 percent believe in life after death, 50 percent believe in human psychic powers, 30 percent think their lives are directly influenced by the position of the stars (and 70 percent follow their horoscopes anyway— just in case), and 20 percent believe they are at risk of being abducted by aliens.[3]

The problem—I mean the problem for children's education—is not just that so many adults positively believe in things that flatly contradict the modern scientific worldview, but that so many do not believe in things that are absolutely central to the scientific view. A survey published last year showed that half the American people do not know, for example, that the earth goes round the sun once a year. Fewer than one in ten know what a molecule is. More than half do not accept that human beings have evolved from animal ancestors, and less than one in ten believe that evolution—if it has occurred—can have taken place without some kind of external intervention. Not only do people not know the results of science, but they do not even know what science is. When asked what they think distinguishes the scientific method, only 2 percent realise it involves putting theories to the test; 34 percent vaguely know it has something to do with experiments and measurement, but 66 percent don't have a clue.[4]

Nor do these figures, worrying as they are, give the full picture of what children are up against. They tell us about the beliefs of typical people and so about the belief environment of the average child. But there are small but significant communities just down the road from us—I mean literally just down the road, in New York, or London, or Oxford—where the situation is arguably very much worse. In these communities, not only are superstition and ignorance even more firmly entrenched but this goes hand in hand with the imposition of repressive regimes of social and interpersonal conduct in relation to hygiene, diet, dress, sex, gender roles, marriage arrangements, and so on. I think, for example, of the Amish Christians, Hasidic Jews, Jehovah's Witnesses, Orthodox Muslims . . . or, for that matter, the radical New Agers . . . all no doubt very different from each other, all with their own peculiar hang-ups and neuroses, but alike in providing an intellectual and cultural dungeon for those who live among them.

In theory, maybe, the children need not suffer. Adults might perhaps keep their beliefs to themselves and not make any active attempt to pass them on. But we know, I'm sure, better than to expect that. This kind of self-restraint is simply not in the nature of a parent-child relationship. If a mother, for example, sincerely believes that eating pork is a sin, or that the best cure for depression is holding a crystal to her head, or that after she dies she will be reincarnated as a mongoose, or that Capricorns and Aries are bound to quarrel, she is hardly likely to withhold such serious matters from her own offspring.

But, more important, as Richard Dawkins has explained so well,[5] this kind of self-restraint is not in the nature of successful belief systems. Belief systems in general flourish or die out according to how good they are at reproduction and competition. The better a system is at creating copies of itself and the better at keeping other rival belief systems at bay, the greater its own chances of evolving and holding its own. So we should expect that it will be characteristic of successful belief systems—especially those that survive when everything else seems to be against them—that their devotees will be obsessed with education and with discipline, insisting on the rightness of their own ways and rubbishing or preventing access to others. We should expect, moreover, that they will make a special point of targeting children in the home, while they are still available, impressionable, and vulnerable. For, as the Jesuit master wisely noted, "If I have the teaching of children up to seven years of age or thereabouts, I care not who has them afterwards, they are mine for life."[6]

Donald Kraybill, an anthropologist who made a close study of an Amish community in Pennsylvania, was well placed to observe how this works out in practice. "Groups threatened by cultural extinction," he writes, "must indoctrinate their offspring if they want to preserve their unique heritage. Socialization of the very young is one of the most potent forms of social control. As cultural values slip into the child's mind, they become personal values—embedded in conscience and governed by emotions. . . . The Amish contend that the Bible commissions parents to train their children in religious matters as well as the Amish way of life. . . . An ethnic nursery, staffed by extended family and church members, moulds the Amish world view in the child's mind from the earliest moments of consciousness."[7]

But what he is describing is not, of course, peculiar to the Amish. "An ethnic nursery, staffed by extended family and church members" could be as much a description of the early environment of a Belfast Catholic, a Birmingham Sikh, a Brooklyn Hasidic Jew—or maybe the child of a North Oxford don. All sects that are serious about their own survival do indeed make every attempt to flood the child's mind with their own propaganda and to deny the child access to any *alternative* viewpoints.

In the United States, this kind of restricted education has continually received the blessing of the law. Parents have the legal right, if they wish to, to educate their children entirely at home, and nearly one million families do so.[8] But many more who wish to limit what their children learn can rely on the thousands of sectarian schools that are permitted to function subject to only minimal state supervision. A U.S. court did recently insist that teachers at a Baptist school should at least hold teaching certificates, but at the same time it recognised that "the whole purpose of such a school is to foster the development of their children's minds in a religious environment" and therefore that the school should be allowed to teach all subjects "in its own way"—which meant, as it happened, presenting all subjects only from a biblical point of view and requiring all teachers, supervisors, and assistants to agree with the church's doctrinal position.[9]

Yet, parents hardly need the support of the law to achieve such a baleful hegemony over their children's minds. There are, unfortunately, many ways of isolating children from external influences without actually physically removing them or controlling what they hear in class. Dress a little boy in the uniform of the Hasidim, curl his side-locks, subject him to strange dietary taboos, make him spend all weekend reading the Torah, tell him that gentiles are dirty, and you could send him to any school in the world and he'd still be a child of the Hasidim. The same—just change the terms a bit—for a child of the Muslims, Roman Catholics, or followers of the Maharishi Yogi.

More worrying still, the children themselves may often be unwitting collaborators in this game of isolation, for children all too easily learn who they are, what is allowed for them, and where they must not go—even in thought. John Schumaker, an Australian psychologist, described his own Catholic boyhood in the following way:

> I believed wholeheartedly that I would burn in eternal fire if I ate meat on a Friday. I now hear that people no longer spend an eternity in fire for eating meat on Fridays. Yet, I cannot help thinking back on the many Saturdays when I rushed to confess about the bologna and ketchup sandwich I could not resist the day before. I usually hoped I would not die before getting to the 3 p.m. confession.[10]

All the same, this particular Catholic boy escaped and lived to tell the tale. In fact, Schumaker became an atheist and has gone on to make something of a profession of his godlessness. Of course, he is not unique. There are plenty of other examples, known to all of us, of men and women who as children were pressured into becoming junior members of a sect—Christian, Jewish, Muslim, Marxist—and yet who came out the other side as free thinkers and seemingly none the worse for their experience.

Then perhaps I am, after all, being too alarmist about what all this means. For surely the *risks* are real enough. We do live—even in our advanced, democratic, Western nations—in an environment of spiritual oppression, where many little children—our neighbours' children if not actually ours—are daily exposed to the attempts of adults to annex their minds. Yet, you may still want to point out that there's a big difference between what the adults want and what actually transpires. All right, so children do frequently get saddled with adult nonsense, but so what? Maybe it's just something the child has to put up with until he or she is able to leave home and learn better. In which case, I would have to admit that the issue is not nearly so serious as I have been making out. After all, you might say, there are surely lots of things that are done to children either accidentally or by design that—though they may not be ideal for the child at the time—have no lasting ill effects.

I'd reply: yes and no. Yes, it's right we should not fall into the error of a previous era of psychology of assuming that people's values and beliefs are determined once and for all by what they learn—or do not learn—as children. The first years of life, though certainly formative, are not necessarily the "critical period" they were once thought to be. Psychologists no longer generally believe that children "imprint" on the first ideas they come across and thereafter refuse to follow any others. In most cases, rather, it seems that individuals can and will remain open to new opportunities of learning later in life—and, if need be, will be able to make up a surprising amount of lost ground in areas where they have earlier been deprived or been misled.[11]

Yes, I agree therefore we should not be *too* alarmist—or too prissy— about the effects of early learning. But, no, we should certainly not be too sanguine about it either. True, it may not be so difficult for a person to unlearn or replace factual knowledge later in life: someone who once thought the world was flat, for example, may, when faced by overwhelming evidence to the contrary, grudgingly come around to accepting that the world is round. It will, however, often be very much more difficult for a person to unlearn established procedures or habits of thought: someone who has grown used, for example, to taking everything on trust from biblical authority may find it very hard indeed to adopt a more critical and questioning attitude. And it may be nigh impossible for a person to unlearn attitudes and emotional reactions: someone who has learned as a child, for example, to think of sex as sinful may never again be able to be relaxed about making love.

But there is another, even more pressing, reason not to be too sanguine or sanguine in the least. Research has shown that *given the opportunity* individuals can go on learning and can recover from poor childhood environments. However, what we should be worrying about are precisely those cases where such opportunities do not—indeed, are not allowed to—occur.

Suppose, as I began to describe above, children are in effect locked out by their families from access to any alternative ideas, or, worse, that they are so effectively immunised against foreign influences that they do the locking out themselves. Think of those cases, not so uncommon, when it has become a central plank of someone's belief system that they must not let themselves be defiled by mixing with others. When, because of their faith, all they want to hear is one voice, and all they want to read is one text. When they treat new ideas as if they carry infection. When, later, as they grow more sophisticated, they come to deride reason as an instrument of Satan. When they regard the humility of unquestioning obedience as a virtue. When they identify ignorance of worldly affairs with spiritual grace. In such cases, it hardly matters what their minds may still remain capable of learning, because they themselves will have made certain they never again use this capacity.

The question was, does childhood indoctrination matter, and the answer, I regret to say, is that it matters more than you might guess. The Jesuit did know what he was saying. Though human beings are remarkably resilient, the truth is that the effects of *well-designed* indoctrination may still prove irreversible, because one of the effects of such indoctrination will be precisely to remove the means and the motivation to reverse it. Several of these belief systems I have been discussing simply could not survive in a free and open market of comparison and criticism, but they have cunningly seen to it that they don't have to by enlisting believers as their own gaolers. So, the bright young lad, full of hope and joy and inquisitiveness, becomes in time the nodding elder buried in the Torah; the little maid, fresh to the morning of the world, becomes the washed-up New Age earth mother lost in mists of superstition.

Yet if this is right, we can ask, what would happen if this kind of vicious circle were to be forcibly broken? What would happen if, for example, there were to be an externally imposed "time-out"? Wouldn't we predict that, just to the extent it *is* a vicious circle, the process of becoming a fully fledged believer might be surprisingly easy to disrupt? I think the clearest evidence of how these belief systems typically hold sway over their followers can in fact be found in historical examples of what has happened when group members have been involuntarily exposed to the fresh air of the outside world.

An interesting test was provided in the 1960s by the case of the Amish and the military draft.[12] The Amish have consistently refused to serve in the armed forces of the United States on grounds of conscience. Until the 1960s, young Amish men who were due to be drafted for military service were regularly granted "agricultural deferments" and were able to continue working safely on their family farms. But as the draft continued through the Vietnam War, an increasing number of these men were deemed ineligible for farm deferments and were required instead to serve two years working in public hospitals—where they were introduced, like it or not, to all manner of non-Amish people and non-Amish ways. Now, when the time came for these men to return home, many no longer wanted to do so and opted to defect. They had tasted the sweets of a more open, adventurous, free-thinking way of life, and they were not about to declare it all a snare and a delusion.

These defections were rightly regarded by Amish leaders as such a serious threat to their culture's survival that they quickly moved to negotiate a special agreement with the government, under which all their draftees could in future be sent to Amish-run farms so that this kind of breach of security should not happen again.

Let me take stock. I have been discussing the survival strategies of some of the more tenacious beliefs systems—the epidemiology, if you like, of those religions and pseudo-religions that Richard Dawkins has called "cultural viruses."[13] But you'll see that, especially with this last ex-

ample, I have begun to approach the next and more important of the issues I wanted to address: the ethical one.

Suppose that, as the Amish case suggests, young members of such a
faith would—if given the opportunity to make up their own minds—
choose to leave. Doesn't this say something important about the morality
of imposing any such faith on children to begin with? I think it does. In
fact, I think it says everything we need to know in order to condemn it.

You'll agree that, if it were female circumcision we were talking about,
we could build a moral case against it based just on considering whether
it is something a woman would choose for herself. Given the fact—I assume it is a fact—that most of those women who were circumcised as
children would, if they only knew what they were missing, have preferred to remain intact. Given that almost no woman who was not circumcised as a child volunteers to undergo the operation later in life.
Given, in short, that it seems not to be what free women want to have
done to their bodies. Then it seems clear that whoever takes advantage of
their temporary power over a child's body to perform the operation must
be abusing this power and acting wrongly.

Well then, if this is so for bodies, the same for minds. Given, let's say,
that most people who have been brought up as members of a sect would,
if they only knew what they are being denied, have preferred to remain
outside it. Given that almost no one who was not brought up this way
volunteers to adopt the faith later in life. Given, in short, that it is not a
faith that a freethinker would adopt. Then, likewise, it seems clear that
whoever takes advantage of their temporary power over a child's mind
to impose this faith is equally abusing this power and acting wrongly.

So I'll come to the main point—and lesson—of this lecture. I want to
propose a general test for deciding when and whether the teaching of a
belief system to children is morally defensible, as follows. If it is ever the
case that teaching this system to children will mean that later in life they
come to hold beliefs that, were they in fact to have had access to alternatives, they would most likely *not* have chosen for themselves, then it is
morally wrong of whoever presumes to impose this system and to *choose
for them* to do so. No one has the right to *choose badly* for anyone else.

This test, I admit, will not be simple to apply. It is rare enough for there
to be the kind of social experiment that occurred with the Amish and the
military draft. And even such an experiment does not actually provide so
strong a test as I'm suggesting we require. After all, the Amish young
men were not offered the alternative until they were already almost
grown up, whereas what we need to know is what the children of the
Amish or any other sect would choose for themselves if they were to
have had access to the full range of alternatives all along. In practice, of
course, such a totally free choice is never going to be available.

Still, utopian as the criterion is, I think its moral implications remain pretty obvious. For, even supposing we cannot know—and can only guess on the basis of weaker tests—whether an individual exercising this genuinely free choice would choose the beliefs that others intend to impose upon him or her, then this state of ignorance in itself must be grounds for making it morally wrong to proceed. In fact, perhaps the best way of putting this is to put it the other way around and say: *only* if we know that teaching a system to children will mean that later in life they come to hold beliefs that, were they to have had access to alternatives, they would *still* have chosen for themselves, only then can it be morally allowable for whoever imposes this system and chooses for them to do so. And in all other cases, the moral imperative must be to hold off.

Now, I expect most of you will probably be happy to agree with this—so far as it goes. Of course, other things being equal, everybody has a right to self-determination of both body and mind—and it must indeed be morally wrong of others to stand in the way of it. But this is: *other things being equal*. And, to continue with those questions I raised earlier, what happens when other things are not equal?

It is surely a commonplace in ethics that sometimes the rights of individuals have to be limited or even overruled in the interests of the larger good or to protect the rights of other people. And it's certainly not immediately obvious why the case of children's intellectual rights should be an exception.

As we saw, there are several factors that might be considered as counterbalances. Of these, the one that seems to many people weightiest or at least is often mentioned first is our interest as a society in maintaining cultural diversity. All right, you may want to say, so it's tough on a child of the Amish or the Hasidim or the Gypsies to be shaped up by their parents in the ways they are—but at least the result is that these fascinating cultural traditions continue. Would not our whole civilisation be impoverished if they were to go? It's a shame, maybe, when individuals have to be sacrificed to maintain such diversity. But there it is: it's the price we pay as a society.

Except, I would feel bound to remind you, *we* do not pay it, *they* do.

Let me give a telling example. In 1995, in the high mountains of Peru, some climbers came across the frozen mummified body of a young Inca girl. She was dressed as a princess. She was thirteen years old. About five hundred years ago, this little girl had, it seems, been taken alive up the mountain by a party of priests and then ritually killed—a sacrifice to the mountain's gods in the hope that they would look kindly on the people below.

The discovery was described by the anthropologist Johan Reinhard in an article for *National Geographic* magazine.[14] He was clearly elated both as a scientist and as a human being by the romance of finding this "ice maiden," as he called her. Even so, he did express some reservations about how she had come to be there: "We can't help but shudder," he wrote, "at [the Incas'] practice of performing human sacrifice."

The discovery was also made the subject of a documentary film shown on American television. Here, however, no one expressed any reservation whatsoever. Instead, viewers were simply invited to marvel at the spiritual commitment of the Inca priests and to share with the girl on her last journey her pride and excitement at having been selected for the signal honor of being sacrificed. The message of the TV programme was, in effect, that the practice of human sacrifice was in its own way a glorious cultural invention—another jewel in the crown of multiculturalism, if you like.

Yet, how dare anyone even suggest this? How dare they invite us—in our sitting rooms, watching television—to feel uplifted by contemplating an act of ritual murder: the murder of a dependent child by a group of stupid, puffed up, superstitious, ignorant old men? How dare they invite us to find good for ourselves in contemplating an immoral action against someone else?

Immoral? By Inca standards? No, that's not what matters. Immoral by ours—and in particular by just the standard of free choice that I was enunciating earlier. The plain fact is that none of *us*, knowing what we do about the way the world works, would freely choose to be sacrificed as she was. And however "proud" the Inca girl may or may not have been to have had the choice made for her by her family (and for all we know, she may actually have felt betrayed and terrified), we can still be pretty sure that she, if she had known what we now know, would not have chosen this fate for herself either.

No, this girl was used by others as a means for achieving their ends. The elders of her community valued their collective security above her life and decided for her that she must die in order that their crops might grow and they might live. Now, five hundred years later, we ourselves must not, in a lesser way, do the same, by thinking of her death as something that enriches *our* collective culture.

We must not do it here, nor in any other case where we are invited to celebrate other people's subjection to quaint and backward traditions as evidence of what a rich world we live in. We mustn't do it even when it can be argued, as I'd agree it sometimes can be, that the maintenance of these minority traditions is potentially of benefit to all of us because they keep alive ways of thinking that might one day serve as a valuable counterpoint to the majority culture.

The U.S. Supreme Court, in supporting the Amish claim to be exempt from sending their children to public schools, commented in an aside:

"We must not forget that in the Middle Ages important values of the civilization of the Western World were preserved by members of religious orders who isolated themselves from all worldly influences against great obstacles."[15] By analogy, the Court implied, we should recognise that the Amish may be preserving ideas and values that our own descendants may one day wish to return to.

But what the Court has failed to recognize is that there is a crucial difference between the religious communities of the Middle Ages, the monks of Holy Island for example, and the present-day Amish: namely, that the monks made their own choice to become monks; they did not have their monasticism imposed on them as children, nor did they in their turn impose it on their own children—for indeed they did not have any. Those mediaeval orders survived by the recruitment of adult volunteers. The Amish, by contrast, survive only by kidnapping little children before they can protest. The Amish may—possibly—have wonderful things to teach the rest of us; and so may—possibly—the Incas have done, and so may several other outlying groups. But these things must not be paid for by the children's lives.

This is, surely, the crux of it. It is a cornerstone of every decent moral system, stated explicitly by Immanuel Kant but already implicit in most people's very idea of morality, that human individuals have an absolute right to be treated as *ends in themselves*—and never as *means* to achieving other people's ends. It goes without saying that this right applies no less to children than to anybody else. And since, in so many situations, children are in no position to look after themselves, it is morally obvious that the rest of us have a particular duty to watch out for them.

So, in every case in which we come across examples of children's lives being manipulated to serve other ends, we have a duty to protest. This duty exists, no matter whether the other ends involve the mollification of the gods, "the preservation of important values for Western civilisation," the creation of an interesting anthropological exhibit for the rest of us, or—now I'll come to the next big question that's been waiting—the fulfillment of certain needs and aspirations of the child's own parents. There is, I'd say, no reason whatever why we should treat the actions of parents as coming under a different set of moral rules here.

The relationship of parent to child is, of course, a special one in all sorts of ways. But it is not so special as to deny the child his or her individual personhood. It is not a relationship of co-extension nor one of ownership. Children are not a part of their parents, nor except figuratively do they "belong" to them. Children are in no sense their parents' private property. Indeed, to quote the U.S. Supreme Court, commenting in a different context on this same issue: it is a "moral fact that a person belongs to himself and not others nor to society as a whole."[16]

It will, therefore, be as much a breach of children's rights if they are used by their parents to achieve the parents' personal goals as it would be if this were done by anyone else. No one has a right to treat children as anything less than ends in themselves.

Still, some of you, I'm sure, will want to argue that the case of parents is not *quite* the same as that of outsiders. No doubt we'd all agree that parents have no more right than anyone else to exploit children for ends that are obviously selfish—to abuse them sexually, for example, or to exploit them as servants, or to sell them into slavery. But, first, isn't it different when the parents at least think their own ends are the child's ends too? When their manipulation of the child's beliefs to conform to theirs is—so as far as they are concerned—entirely in the child's best interests? And then, second, isn't it different when the parents have already invested so much of their own resources in the child, giving him or her so much of their love and care and time? Haven't they somehow earned the reward of having the child honor their beliefs, even if these beliefs are—by other people's lights—eccentric or old-fashioned? Don't these considerations, together, mean that parents have at least some rights that other people don't have, rights that arguably should come before—or at least rank beside—the rights of the children themselves?

No. The truth is these considerations simply don't add up to any form of *rights*, let alone rights that could outweigh the children's: at most they merely provide mitigating circumstances. Imagine. Suppose you were misguidedly to give your own child poison. The fact that you might think the poison you were administering was good for your child, that you might have gone to a lot of trouble to obtain this poison, and that if it were not for all your efforts your child would not have even been there to be offered it, none of this would give you *a right* to administer the poison—at most, it would only make you less culpable when the child died.

But in any case, to see the parents as simply misguided about the child's true interests is, I think, to put too generous a construction on it. For it is not at all clear that parents, when they take control of their children's spiritual and intellectual lives, really do believe they are acting in the child's best interests rather than their own. When Abraham was commanded by God on the mountain to kill his son, Isaac, and dutifully went ahead with the preparation, he was surely not thinking of what was best for Isaac—he was thinking of his own relationship with God. And so on down the ages. Parents have used and still use their children to bring *themselves* spiritual or social benefits: dressing them up, educating them, baptising them, and bringing them to confirmation or Bar Mitzvah in order to maintain their own social and religious standing.

Consider again the analogy with circumcision. No one should make the mistake of supposing that female circumcision, in those places where it's practised, is done to benefit the girl. Rather, it is done for the honor of the family, to demonstrate the parents' commitment to a tradition, and to save them from dishonor. Although I would not push the analogy too far, I think the motivation of the parents is not so different at many other levels of parental manipulation—even when it comes to such apparently unselfish acts as deciding what a child should or should not learn in school.

A Christian fundamentalist mother, for example, forbids her child to attend classes on evolution: though she may claim she is doing it for the child and not, of course, herself, she is very likely motivated primarily by a desire to make a display of her own purity. Doesn't she just know that God is mighty proud of her for conforming to his will? The chief mullah of Saudi Arabia proclaims that the Earth is flat and that anyone who teaches otherwise is a friend of Satan: won't he himself be thrice blessed by Allah for making this courageous stand? A group of rabbis in Jerusalem try to ban the showing of the film *Jurassic Park* on the grounds that it may give children the idea that there were dinosaurs living on earth 60 million years ago, when the scriptures state that in fact the world is just 6,000 years old: are they not making a wonderful public demonstration of their own piety?[17]

What we are seeing, as often as not, is pure self-interest. In which case, we should not even allow a mitigating plea of good intentions on the part of the parent or other responsible adult. They are looking after none other than themselves.

Yet, as I said, in the end it hardly matters what the parents' intentions are. Because even the best of intentions would not be sufficient to buy them "parental rights" over their children. Indeed, the very idea that parents or any other adults have "rights" *over* children is morally insupportable. No human being, in any other circumstances, is credited with having rights *over* anyone else. No one is entitled, as of right, to control, use, or direct the life course of another person—even for objectively good ends. It's true that in the past slaveowners had such legal rights over their slaves. And it's true too that, until comparatively recently, the anomaly persisted of husbands having certain such rights over their wives—the right to have sex with them, for instance. But neither of these exceptions provides a good model for regulating parent-child relationships.

Children, to repeat, have to be considered as having interests independent of their parents. They cannot be subsumed as if they were part of the same person. At least, so it should be. Unless, that is, we make the extraordinary mistake that the U.S. Supreme Court apparently did when it ruled, in relation to the Amish, that although the Amish way of life may be considered "odd or even erratic," it "interferes with no rights or interests of *others*" (my italics).[18] As if the children of the Amish are not even to be counted as potentially "others."

I think we should stop talking of "parental rights" at all. Insofar as they compromise the child's rights as an individual, parents' rights have no status in ethics and should have none in law.[19] This is not to say that, other things being equal, parents should not be treated by the rest of us with due respect and accorded certain "privileges" in relation to their children. "Privileges," however, do not have the same legal or moral significance as rights. Privileges are by no means unconditional, they come as the quid pro quo for agreeing to abide by certain rules of conduct imposed by society at large, and anyone to whom a privilege is granted remains, in effect, on probation: a privilege granted can be taken away.

For example, let's suppose that the privilege of parenting will mean that, provided parents agree to act within an agreed framework, they shall indeed be allowed—without interference from the law—to do all the things that parents everywhere usually do: feeding, clothing, educating, disciplining their own children, and enjoying the love and creative involvement that follow from these activities. But it will explicitly *not* be part of this deal that parents should be allowed to offend against the child's more fundamental rights to self-determination. If parents do abuse their privileges in this regard, the contract lapses—and it is then the duty of those who granted the privilege to intervene.

Intervene *how*? Suppose we—I mean we as a society—do not like what is happening when the education of a child has been left to parents or priests. Suppose we fear for the child's mind and want to take remedial action. Suppose, indeed, we want to take preemptive action with *all* children to protect them from being hurt by bad ideas and to give them the best possible start as thoughtful human beings. What should we be doing about it? What should be our birthday present to them from the grown-up world?

My suggestion at the start of this paper was science—universal scientific education. That is to say, education in learning from observation, experiment, hypothesis testing, constructive doubt, critical thinking, and the truths that flow from these processes.

And so I've come at last to the most provocative of the questions I began with. What's so special about science? Why *these* truths? Why should it be morally right to teach *this* to everybody, when it's apparently so morally wrong to teach all those other things?

You do not have to be one of those out-and-out relativists to raise such questions and to be suspicious that any attempt to replace the old truths by newer scientific truths might be nothing other than an attempt to replace one dogmatism by another. The Supreme Court, in its judgment about Amish schooling, was careful to warn that we should never rule out one way of thinking and rule another in merely on the basis of what happens to be the modern, fashionable opinion. "There can be no assumption," it said, "that today's majority is 'right' and the Amish and others are 'wrong'"; the Amish way of life "is not to be condemned because it is different."[20]

Maybe so. And yet I'd say the Court has chosen to focus on the wrong issue there. Even if science *were* the "majority" worldview (which, as we saw earlier, is sadly not the case), we'd all agree that this in itself would provide no grounds for promoting science above other systems of thought. The "majority" is clearly not right about lots of things, probably most things.

But the grounds I'm proposing are firmer. Some of the other speakers in this lecture series will have talked about the values and virtues of science. And I am sure they too, in their own terms, will have attempted to explain why science is different—why it ought to have a unique claim on our heads and on our hearts. But I will now perhaps go even further than they would. I think science stands apart from and superior to all other systems for the reason that it alone of all the systems in contention meets the criterion I laid out above: namely, that it represents a set of beliefs that reasonable people would, if given the chance, choose for themselves.

I should probably say that again and put it in context. I argued earlier that the only circumstances under which it should be morally acceptable to impose a particular way of thinking on children are when the result will be that later in life they come to hold beliefs that they would have chosen anyway, no matter what alternative beliefs they were exposed to. And what I am now saying is that science is the one way of thinking—maybe the only one—that passes this test. There is a fundamental asymmetry between science and everything else.

What do you reckon? Let's go to the rescue of that Inca girl who is being told by the priests that, unless she dies on the mountain, the gods will rain down lava on her village, and let's offer her another way of looking at things. Offer her a choice as to how she will grow up: on one side with this story about divine anger, or on the other side with the insights from geology as to how volcanoes arise from the movement of tectonic plates. Which will she choose to follow?

Let's go help the Muslim boy who's being schooled by the mullahs into believing that the earth is flat, and let's explore some of the ideas of scientific geography with him. Better still, let's take him up high in a balloon, show him the horizon, and invite him to use his own senses and powers of reasoning to reach his own conclusions. Now, offer him the choice: the picture presented in the book of the Koran or the one that flows from his newfound scientific understanding. Which will he prefer?

Or let's take pity on the Baptist teacher who has become wedded to creationism, and let's give her a vacation. Let's walk her round the natural history museum in the company of Richard Dawkins or Daniel Dennett—or, if they're too scary, David Attenborough—and let's have them explain the possibilities of evolution to her. Now, offer her the choice: the story of Genesis with all its paradoxes and special pleading or the startlingly simple idea of natural selection. Which will she choose?

My questions are rhetorical because the answers are already in. We know very well which way people will go when they really are allowed to make up their own minds on questions such as these. Conversions from superstition to science have been and are everyday events. They have probably been part of our personal experience. Those who have been walking in darkness have seen a great light—the aha! of scientific revelation.

By contrast, conversions from science back to superstition are virtually unknown. It just does not happen that someone who has learnt and understood science and its methods and who is then offered a nonscientific alternative chooses to abandon science. I doubt there has ever been a case, for example, of someone who has been brought up to believe the geological theory of volcanoes moving over to believing in divine anger instead, or of someone who has seen and appreciated the evidence that the world is round reverting to the idea that the world is flat, or even of someone who has once understood the power of Darwinian theory going back to preferring the story of Genesis.

People do, of course, sometimes abandon their existing scientific beliefs in favor of newer and better scientific alternatives. But to choose one scientific theory over another is still to remain absolutely true to science.

The reason for this asymmetry between science and nonscience is not—at least not only—that science provides so much better—so much more economical, elegant, and beautiful—explanations than nonscience. Although there is that. The still stronger reason, I'd suggest, is that science is by its very nature a participatory process, and nonscience is not.

In learning science, we learn *why we should believe* this or that. Science doesn't cajole, and it doesn't dictate; it lays out the factual and theoretical arguments as to why something is so—and invites us to assent to them, to see it for ourselves. Hence, by the time someone has understood a scientific explanation, they have in an important sense already chosen it as theirs.

How different is the case of religious or superstitious explanation. Religion makes no pretence of engaging its devotees in any process of rational discovery or choice. If we dare ask *why* we should believe something, the answer will be because it has been written in the book, because this is our tradition, because it was good enough for Moses, because you'll go to heaven that way. Or, as often as not, don't ask.

Contrast these two positions. On one side there is the second-century Roman theologian Tertullian, with his abject submission to authority and denial of our personal involvement in choosing our beliefs. "For us," he wrote, "curiosity is no longer necessary after Jesus Christ nor inquiry after the Gospel."[21] This is the same man, I might remind you, who said of Christianity: "It is certain because it is impossible." On the other side, there is the twelfth-century English philosopher Adelard of Bath, one of the earliest interpreters of Arab science, with his injunction that we all make ourselves personally responsible for understanding what goes on around us. "If anyone living in a house is ignorant of what it is made, . . . he is unworthy of its shelter," he said, "and if anyone born in the residence of this world neglects learning the plan underlying its marvellous beauty . . . he is unworthy, and deserves to be cast out of it."[22]

Imagine that the choice is yours. That you have been faced, in the formative years of your life, with a choice between these two paths to enlightenment—between basing your beliefs on the ideas of others imported from another country and another time and basing them on ideas that you have been able to see growing in your home soil. Can there be any doubt that you will choose for yourself, that you will choose science?

And because people will so choose, *if* they have the opportunity of scientific education, I say we as a society are entitled with good conscience to *insist* on their being given that opportunity. That is, we are entitled in effect to choose this way of thinking for them. Indeed we are not just entitled: in the case of children, we are morally obliged to do so—so as to protect them from being early victims of other ways of thinking that would remove them from the field.

Then—let me catch the question from the back of the hall—"How'd *you* like it if some Big Brother were to insist on *your* children being taught *his* beliefs? How'd you like it if *I* tried to impose my personal ideology on *your* little girl?" I have the answer: that teaching science isn't like that, it's not about teaching someone else's beliefs, it's about encouraging the child to exercise her powers of understanding to arrive at her own beliefs.

For sure, this is likely to mean she will end up with beliefs that are widely shared with others who have taken the same path: beliefs, that is, in what science reveals as the *truth* about the world. And yes, if you want to put it this way, you could say this means that by her own efforts at understanding, she will have become a scientific conformist: one of those predictable people who believes that matter is made of atoms, that the universe arose with the Big Bang, that humans are descended from monkeys, that consciousness is a function of the brain, that there is no life after death, and so on. But since you ask, I'll say I'd be only too pleased if a big brother or sister or schoolteacher, or you yourself, sir, should help her get to that enlightened state.

The habit of questioning, the ability to tell good answers from bad, an appetite for seeing how and why deep explanations work—such is what

I would want for my daughter (now two years old) because I think it is what she, given the chance, would one day want for herself. But it is also what I would want for her because I am too well aware of what might otherwise befall her. Bad ideas continue to swill through our culture, some old, some new, looking for receptive minds to capture. If this girl, because she were to lack the defences of critical reasoning, were ever to fall prey to some kind of political or spiritual irrationalism, then I and you—and our society—would have failed her.

Words? Children are made of the words they hear. It matters what we tell them. They can be hurt by words. They may go on to hurt themselves still further and in turn become the kind of people that hurt others. But they can be given life by words as well.

"I have set before you life and death, blessing and cursing,"—these are the words of Deuteronomy—"therefore choose life, that both thou and thy seed may live."[23] I think there should be no limit to our duty to help children to choose life.

Notes

Amnesty Lecture, Sheldonian Theatre, Oxford, 21st February 1997. I am indebted for several of the ideas here to James Dwyer, whose critique of the idea of parents' rights stands as a model of philosophical and legal reasoning.

1. Christopher Cherniak, "The Riddle of the Universe and Its Solution," in Douglas R. Hofstadter and Daniel C. Dennett, eds., *The Mind's I* (New York: Basic Books, 1981), pp. 269–276.

2. Vladimir Mayakovsky, "I," in *Mayakovsky and His Poetry*, trans. George Reavey (1912; reprint, Bombay: Current Book House, 1955).

3. Statistics from sources quoted in Nicholas Humphrey, *Soul Searching: Human Nature and Supernatural Belief* (London: Chatto and Windus, 1995).

4. National Science Board, *Science and Engineering Indicators—1996* (Washington, D.C.: U.S. Government Printing Office, 1996).

5. Richard Dawkins, *The Selfish Gene* (Oxford: Oxford University Press, 1976), chap. 11.

6. Jesuit divine (apocryphal).

7. Donald B. Kraybill, *The Riddle of Amish Culture* (Baltimore: Johns Hopkins University Press, 1989), p. 119.

8. "Home Schools: How Do They Affect Children?" *APA Monitor* (December 1996).

9. Court ruling Iowa, 1985, cited by James G. Dwyer, "Parents' Religion and Children's Welfare: Debunking the Doctrine of Parents' Rights," *California Law Review* 82 (1994), pp. 1371–1447.

10. John F. Schumaker, *Wings of Illusion* (London: Polity Press, 1990), p. 33.

11. See, for example, the review by Jerome Kagan, "Three Pleasing Ideas," *American Psychologist* 51 (1996), pp. 901–908.

12. Kraybill, *The Riddle of Amish Culture*, p. 218.

13. Richard Dawkins, "Viruses of the Mind," in B. Dahlbom, ed., *Dennett and His Critics* (Oxford: Blackwell, 1993), pp. 13–27.

14. Johan Reinhard, "Peru's Ice Maidens," *National Geographic* (June 1996).

15. Supreme Court ruling, *Wisconsin v. Yoder,* 406 U.S., 1972, cited by Dwyer, "Parents' Religion and Children's Welfare: Debunking the Doctrine of Parents' Rights," *California Law Review* 82 (1994), p. 1385.

16. Supreme Court ruling, *Thornburgh v. American College of Obstetricians and Gynecologists,* 476 U.S., 1986, cited by Dwyer, "Parents' Religion and Children's Welfare: Debunking the Doctrine of Parents' Rights," *California Law Review* 82 (1994), p. 1409.

17. The examples cited here are taken from Carl Sagan, *The Demon-Haunted World* (New York: Headline, 1996), pp. 304–305.

18. Supreme Court, *Wisconsin v. Yoder*, 406 U.S., 1972, cited by Donald B. Kraybill, *The Riddle of Amish Culture* (Baltimore: Johns Hopkins University Press, 1989), p. 120.

19. See the extended discussion by J. Dwyer, "Parents' Religion and Children's Welfare"; "The Children We Abandon: Religious Exemptions to Child Welfare and Education Laws as Denials of Equal Protection to Children of Religious Objectors," *North Carolina Law Review* 74 (1996), pp. 101–258.

20. Supreme Court, *Wisconsin v. Yoder*, 406 U.S., 1972, cited by Donald B. Kraybill, *The Riddle of Amish Culture* (Baltimore: Johns Hopkins University Press, 1989), p. 120. [The transcript of the Supreme Court decision is reproduced as an appendix to Albert Klein, ed., *Compulsory Education and the Amish* (Boston: Beacon, 1975), pp. 149–181.–Ed.]

21. Tertullian, 2nd century, *The Prescription of Heretics,* xiv, 8.

22. Adelard of Bath, twelfth century, *Astrolabium,* preface.

23. Deuteronomy 30:19.

5

Is the World Simple
or Complex?

John D. Barrow

The view of the Universe created by discoveries in fundamental science has become increasingly influential beyond the halls of science. It provides the basis for many attempts to interpret the significance of the cosmos and the place of humans within it. Whether we like it or not, our scientific picture of the Universe provokes us to make an evaluation of that picture. Until quite recently, that picture was biased by a particular perspective on the workings of Nature, a perspective that was imposed upon us largely by practicalities. In what follows, I take a look at two contrasting views of Nature that have both been much in the news over recent years, as scientists from very different disciplines have trumpeted dramatic developments through the media and in works of popular science. For the outsider, these different messages can be confusing and disjointed. On the one hand, there are the physicists talking of "Theories of Everything" and the rapid convergence of investigations of Nature towards a single, all-encompassing mathematical theory, whereas, on the other hand, we are told of chaos, unpredictability, and bottomless complexity all around us.

These differing messages have each inspired extrapolations into the philosophy of science and other subjects as well, as commentators seek to evaluate what they have to tell us about who we are, why we are, and where we might be going. My aim, here, is one of explanation: to ask whether the Universe is simple or complicated and to show that the question is a subtle one. Its answer takes us on a tour of many important developments in science. Perhaps it will also help us evaluate the significance of these developments—to understand more accurately both their value for science and the forms of value of which science can legitimately speak.

The Ordinary Scientist in the Street

If you were to engage some particle physicists in a conversation about the nature of the world, they might soon be regaling you with a story about how simple and symmetrical the world really is, if only you look at things in the right way. But, when you return to contemplate the real world, you know that it is far from simple. Nor would many other scientists agree with the verdict of the particle physicists. For the psychologist, the economist, the botanist, or the zoologist, the world is anything but simple. It is a higgledy-piggledy of complex events whose nature owes more to their persistence over time, in competition with other alternatives, than to any mysterious penchant for symmetry or simplicity. So who is right? Is the world really simple, as the particle physicists claim, or is it as complex as everyone else seems to think?

Simplicity

Our belief in the simplicity of Nature springs from the observation that there appear to exist "laws" of Nature. The idea of laws of Nature has a long history rooted in monotheistic religious thinking and in practices of social government. This civil and theological background and its history still have a bearing on the values to which science holds today.[1] For our present purposes, it is most instructive to consider the concept of scientific law and order not merely in terms of this ideological history but in the broadest context. To do so, we must understand certain developments in mathematics and computer science that provide some discrimination between order and randomness.

Suppose you encounter two sequences of digits. The first has the form:

.000100010001000100010001. . . .

whereas the second has the form:

. . . 01000101101011111010010. . . .

Now suppose you are asked if these sequences are random or ordered. Clearly, the first appears to be ordered. The reason you say this is because it is possible to "see" a pattern in it; that is, we can replace the sequence by a rule that allows us to remember it or convey it to others without simply listing its contents. In line with this, we will call a sequence *nonrandom* if it can be abbreviated by a formula or a rule shorter than itself. If this is so, we say that it is compressible.[2] By contrast, if, as appears to be the case for the second sequence (which was generated by tossing a coin), there is no abbreviated formula, pattern, or rule that can capture its information content, then we say that it is *incompressible*. If we want to tell our friends about the incompressible sequence, then we simply have to list it in full. There is no encapsulation of its information content shorter than itself.

This simple idea allows us to draw some lessons about the scientific search for a Theory of Everything.[3] We might define science to be the search for compressions. We observe the world in all possible ways and gather facts about it; but although this is necessary for science, it is not sufficient for science. We are not content, like some manic historian, simply to gather up a record of everything that has ever happened. Instead, like real historians, we look for patterns in those facts, compressions of the information on offer; it is those patterns that we value and have come to call the laws of Nature. The search for a Theory of Everything is the quest for an ultimate compression of the world. Interestingly, Greg Chaitin's proof of Kurt Gödel's incompleteness theorem, using the concepts of complexity and compression, reveals that Gödel's theorem is equivalent to the fact that one cannot prove a sequence to be incompressible.[4] We can never prove a compression to be the ultimate one; there might still be a deeper and simpler unification waiting to be found.

Our discussion of the compressibility of sequences has taught us that pattern, or symmetry, is equivalent to laws or rules of change.[5] Classical laws of change, like Newton's laws of motion, are equivalent to the invariance of some quantity or pattern. These equivalences only became known long after the formulation of the laws of motion, which prescribe the allowed changes in terms of causes and effects. This approach strikes a chord with the traditional Platonic tradition, which places emphasis upon the unchanging, atemporal aspects of the world as the key to its fundamental structures. These timeless attributes, or "forms" as Plato called them, seem to have evolved, with the passage of time, into the laws of Nature and the invariances and conserved quantities (like energy and momentum) of modern physics.

Since 1973, when the discovery of asymptotic freedom (the fact that interaction strengths weaken as energy increases) launched particle physicists along a successful line of inquiry, this focus upon symmetry has taken centre stage in the study of elementary particle physics and the laws governing the fundamental interactions of Nature. Symmetry is now taken as the primary guide into the structure of the elementary particle world, and the laws of change are derived from the requirement that particular symmetries, often of a highly abstract character, be preserved. Such theories are called "gauge theories." The currently successful theories of four known forces of Nature—the electromagnetic, weak, strong, and gravitational forces—are all gauge theories. These theories require the existence of the forces they govern in order to preserve the invariances upon which they are based; they are also able to dictate the character of the elementary particles of matter that they govern. In these respects, gauge theories differ from the classical laws of Newton, which, since they governed the motions of all particles, could say nothing about the properties of those particles. The reason for this added power of explanation is that the elementary particle world, in contrast to the macroscopic world, is populated by collections of identical particles ("once you've seen one electron you've seen 'em all," as Richard Feynman once remarked). Particular gauge theories govern the behavior of particular subsets of all the elementary particles, according to their attributes.[6]

The use of symmetry in this powerful way enables entire systems of natural laws to be derived from the requirement that a certain abstract pattern be invariant in the Universe. Subsequently, the predictions of this system of laws can be compared with the actual course of Nature. This is the opposite route to that which was followed a century ago. Then, the systematic study of events would have led to systems of mathematical equations giving the laws of cause and effect. Only later would the fact that these rules of change are equivalent to the requirement that some other quantity does not change be recognised.

This generation of theories for each of the separate interactions of Nature has motivated the search for a unification of those theories into more comprehensive editions based upon larger symmetries. Within those larger patterns, smaller symmetries respected by the individual forces of Nature might be accommodated in an interlocking fashion that places some new constraint upon their allowed forms. So far, this strategy has resulted in a successful, experimentally tested unification of the electromagnetic and weak interactions, as well as a number of purely theoretical proposals for a further unification with the strong interaction ("grand unification") and candidates for a fourfold unification with the gravitational force that would produce a so-called Theory of Everything (TOE).

A favored candidate for a TOE is a variant of "superstring" theory, first developed by Michael Green and John Schwarz.[7] Elementary descriptions of its workings can be found elsewhere.[8] Suffice it to say that the enormous interest that these theories attracted over the past nine years can be attributed to the fact that they revealed that the requirement of logical self-consistency—previously suspected of being a rather weak constraint upon a TOE—turned out to be enormously restrictive. At first, it was believed that it narrowed the alternative down to just two possible symmetries underlying the TOE. Subsequently, the situation has been found to be rather more complicated than first imagined, and superstring theories have been found to require new types of mathematics for their elucidation. Superficially, there appear to be a large number of different superstring theories, but it begins to look as if they are just different mathematical representations of a small number of theories—or even just one theory.

The important lesson to be learned from this part of our discussion is that Theories of Everything, as currently conceived, are simply attempts to encapsulate all the laws governing the fundamental forces of Nature within a single law of Nature derived from the preservation of a single overarching symmetry. I might add that, at present, four fundamental forces are known, of which the weakest is gravitation. There might exist other, far weaker, forces of Nature. Although too weak for us to measure (perhaps ever), their existence may be necessary to fix the logical necessity of that single Theory of Everything. Without any means to check on their existence, we would always be missing a crucial piece of the cosmic jigsaw puzzle. It is this general pattern of explanation in terms of a smaller number of laws governing the fundamental force fields of Nature, culminating in a single unified law, that lies at the heart of the physicist's perception of the world as "simple."

There is a further point that I might raise regarding the quest for a Theory of Everything—if it exists. We might wonder whether such a theory is buried deep (perhaps infinitely deep) in the nature of the Universe, or whether it lies rather shallow. If it lies deep below the present appearances of things, then it would be a most anti-Copernican overconfidence to expect that we would be able to fathom it after just a few hundred years of serious study of the laws of Nature, aided by limited observations of the world by relatively few individuals. There appears to be no good evolutionary reason why our intellectual capabilities need be so great as to unravel the ultimate laws of Nature, unless those ultimate laws are simply a vast elaboration of very simple principles, like counting or comparing, which are employed in local laws.[9] Of course, the unlikelihood of our success does not deprive the effort of its value; nor is it a reason not to try. We just should not have unrealistic expectations about the chances of success or the magnitude of the task.

Complexity

The simplicity and economy of the laws that govern Nature's fundamental forces are not the end of the story, for when we look around us, we do not observe the laws of Nature; rather, we see the *outcomes* of those laws. There is a world of difference. Outcomes are much more complicated than the laws that govern them because they do not have to respect the symmetries displayed by the laws. By this means, it is possible to have a world that displays complicated asymmetrical structures yet is governed by very simple, symmetrical laws. Consider the following simple example. Suppose I balance a ball at the apex of a cone. If I were to release the ball, then the law of gravitation will determine its subsequent motion. But gravity has no preference for any particular direction in the Universe; it is entirely democratic in that respect. Yet, when I release the ball, it will always fall in some particular direction, either because it was given a little push in one direction or as a result of quantum fluctuations which do not permit an unstable equilibrium state to persist. So here, in the outcome of the falling ball, the directional symmetry of the law of gravity is broken. Take another example. You and I are, at this moment, situated at particular places in the Universe, despite the fact that the laws of Nature display no preference for any one place in the Universe over any other. We are both (very complicated) outcomes of the laws of Nature, which break their underlying symmetries with respect to positions in space. This teaches us why science is often so difficult. When we observe the world, we see only the broken symmetries manifested as the outcomes of the laws of Nature; from them, we must work backwards to unmask the hidden symmetries that characterise the laws behind the appearances.

We can now understand the answers that we obtained from the different scientists in the street. The particle physicist works closest to the laws of Nature themselves and so is especially impressed by their simplicity and symmetry. That is the basis for his assertion about the simplicity of Nature. But the biologist or the meteorologist is occupied with the study of the complex outcomes of the laws, rather than with the laws themselves. As a result, she is most impressed by the complexities of Nature rather than by her laws.

The left-hand column in Figure 5.1 represents the development of the Platonic perspective on the world, with its emphasis upon the unchanging elements behind things—laws, conserved quantities, symmetries—whereas the right-hand column, with its stress upon time and change and the concatenation of complex happenings, is the fulfillment of the Aristotelian approach to understanding the world. Until rather recently, physicists have focused almost exclusively upon the study of the laws rather than the complex outcomes. This is not surprising because the study of the outcomes is a far more difficult problem that requires the existence of powerful interactive computers with good graphics for its full implementation. It is no coincidence that the study of complexity and chaos in that world of outcomes has advanced hand in hand with the growing power and availability of low-cost personal computers.[10]

We see that the structure of the world around us cannot be explained by the laws of Nature alone. The broken symmetries around us may not allow us to deduce the underlying laws, and a knowledge of those laws may not allow us to deduce the permitted outcomes. Indeed, the latter state of affairs is not uncommon in fundamental physics and is displayed by the current state of superstring theories. Theoretical physi-

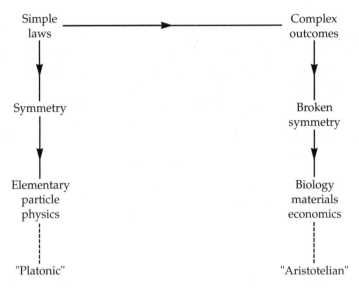

FIGURE 5.1   The Platonic and Aristotelian Approaches to the Study of Nature

cists believe they have the laws (that is, the mathematical equations), but they are unable at present to deduce the outcomes of those laws (that is, find the solutions to those equations). This division of things into laws and outcomes reveals why it is that, although Theories of Everything may be necessary to understand the world we see around us, they are far from sufficient. They are valuable but are not values in themselves.

Of those complex outcomes of the laws of Nature, much the most interesting are those that display what has become known as *organised complexity*. A selection of these are displayed in Figure 5.2, in terms of their size (gauged by information storage capacity) versus their ability to process information (the rate at which they can change one list of numbers into another list).

Increasingly complex entities arise as we proceed up the diagonal, where increasing information storage capability grows hand in hand with the ability to transform that information into new forms. These complex systems are typified by the presence of feedback, self-organisation, and nonequilibrium behavior. There might be no limit to the complexity of the entities that can exist farther and farther up the diagonal. Thus, for example, a complex phenomenon like high-temperature superconductivity, which relies upon a very particular mixture of materials brought together under special conditions, might never have been manifested in the Universe before the right mixtures were made on Earth in 1987.[11] It is most unlikely that these mixtures occur naturally in the Uni-

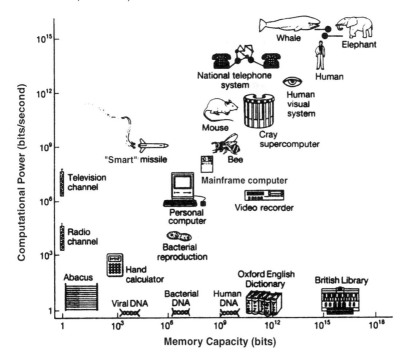

FIGURE 5.2 The Power and Information Storage Capacity of a Variety of Complex Natural and Artificial Structures

verse, and thus that variety of complexity called "high-temperature superconductivity" relies upon that other complexity called "intelligence" to act as a catalyst and midwife for its creation. We might speculate that there exist new types of "laws" or "principles" that govern the existence and evolution of complexity defined in some abstract sense.[12] These rules might be quite different from the laws of the particle physicist; they might not be based upon symmetry and invariance but upon principles of logic and information processing. Perhaps the second law of thermodynamics is as close as we have got to discovering this collection of rules that govern the development of order and disorder.

The defining characteristic of the structures in Figure 5.2 is that they are more than the sum of their parts. They are what they are, they display the behavior that they do, not because they are made of atoms or molecules but because of the way in which their constituents are organised.[13] It is the circuit diagram of the neural network that is responsible for the complexity of its behavior. The laws of electromagnetism alone are insufficient to explain the working of a brain. We need to know how it is wired up and interconnected. No Theory of Everything that the particle physicists supply is likely to shed any light upon the workings of the human brain or the nervous system of an elephant.

On the Edge of Chaos

Until quite recently, sciences like physics emphasised the deduction and confirmation of the laws and regularities of the world. The teaching of science was built around simple, soluble problems that could be dealt with using pencil and paper. During the last decade, there has been a change. The advent of small, inexpensive, powerful computers with good interactive graphics has enabled large, complex, and disordered situations to be studied observationally—by looking at a computer monitor.

Experimental mathematics has been invented. A computer can be programmed to simulate the evolution of complicated systems, and their long-term behavior can be observed, studied, modified, and replayed. It is now possible to construct virtual realities obeying laws of Nature that are not our own and simply explore the consequences. By these means, the study of chaos and complexity has become a subculture within science. The study of the simple, exactly soluble, problems of science has been augmented by a growing appreciation of the vast complexity expected in situations where many competing influences are at work. Prime candidates are supplied by systems that evolve in their environment by natural selection and, in so doing, modify those environments in complicated ways.

As our appreciation for the nuances of chaotic behavior has matured by exposure to natural examples, novelties have emerged. Chaos and order have been found to coexist in a curious symbiosis. Imagine a very large egg timer in which sand is falling, grain by grain, to create a growing sand pile. The pile evolves in an erratic manner. Sandfalls of all sizes occur, and their effect is to maintain the overall gradient of the sand pile in equilibrium, just on the verge of collapse. This self-sustaining process has been dubbed "self-organising criticality" by its discoverer, the Danish physicist Per Bak.[14]

At a microscopic level, the fall of sand is chaotic. If there is nothing peculiar about the sand, which renders avalanches of one size more or less probable than others, then the frequency with which avalanches occur is proportional to some mathematical power of their size (the avalanches are said to be "scale-free" processes). Order develops on a large scale through the combination of many chaotic small-scale events that hover on the brink of instability. The sand pile is always critically poised, and the next avalanche could be of any size, but the effect of the avalanches is to maintain a well-defined overall slope of sand.

The egg timer is but one example among many systems, both natural—like earthquakes—and man-made—like stock market crashes—in which a concatenation of local processes combine to maintain a semblance of equilibrium. Indeed, the course of life on planet Earth might even turn out to be described by such a picture. The chain of living creatures maintains an overall balance despite the constant impact of extinctions, changes of habitat, disease, and disaster that conspire to create local "avalanches." Occasional extinctions open up new niches and allow diversity to flourish anew, until equilibrium is temporarily reestablished. A picture of the living world poised in critical state, in which local chaos sustains global stability, is Nature's subtlest compromise. Complex adaptive systems thrive in the hinterland between the inflexibilities of determinism and the vagaries of chaos. There, they get the best of both worlds: out of chaos springs a wealth of alternatives for natural selection to sift; in the meantime, the rudder of determinism sets a clear average course towards islands of stability.

I have introduced these ideas to highlight a change of scientific perspective on the world, which for so long emphasised the regularities and commonalities behind the appearances. This search for simplicity and order under the assumption of common laws that link the present to the future and the past, has directed the development of science during the last three hundred years. But complexity is not so simple. Only with the coming of new studies of the complex, by means provided by new technologies, has science appreciated the problem of explaining diversity, asymmetry, and irregularity.

The Sound of Music

In what ways do the changes in scientific perspective outlined above bear on a discussion of the values of science? Rather than asking, in absolute terms, whether the world is really simple or complex, it seems more productive to ask if there might not be certain structures, some natural, others man-made, which we value more than others. For if we have evolved to cope with the changing patterns of a complex environment, there may be naturally occurring forms of complexity that our brains are best adapted to apprehend. In such circumstances, artistic appreciation might emerge as a by-product of those adaptations. An interesting aspect of our appreciation of sound has recently come to light, which suggests a way in which such adaptation and evolution might occur.[15]

Physicists and engineers refer to all sequences of sound as noises. A useful way to distinguish and analyse them is by measuring their *spectrum*, which is a measure of the distribution of intensity over different sound frequencies. An important feature of many noise spectra is that they are proportional to a mathematical power of the sound wave frequency over a very wide range of frequencies. In this case, there is no

special frequency that characterises the process—as would result from repeatedly playing the note with the frequency of middle C, for instance.
Such processes are called scale-free (as was the sand pile). If one halves
or doubles all the frequencies, then a scale-free spectrum would keep the
same shape. In a scale-free process, whatever happens in one frequency
range happens in all frequency ranges.

Scale-free processes have spectra that are proportional to inverse powers of the frequency, $1/f^a$, where a is any positive number. The character
of the noise changes significantly according to the value of the constant a.
If noise is entirely random so that every sound is completely independent of its predecessors, then a is zero, and the process is called "white
noise." Like the spectral mixture that we call white light, white noise is
acoustically "colorless"—equally anonymous, featureless, and unpredictable at all frequencies and hence at whatever speed it is played.
When your TV picture goes haywire, the "snow" that blitzes the screen is
a visual display of white noise that arises from the random motion of the
electrons in the circuitry. At low intensities, white noise has a soothing effect because of its lack of discernible correlations. Consequently, white
noise machines are marketed to produce restful background "noise" that
resembles the sound of gently breaking waves. Looked at from another
perspective, white noise is invariably "surprising," in the sense that the
next sound cannot be anticipated from its predecessor. There are no correlations with earlier times.

By contrast, a scale-free noise with a frequency in which $a = 2$ produces
a far more correlated sequence of sounds, called "brown noise." This sequence is also rather unenticing to the ear; its high degree of correlation
gives it a rather predictable development, like going up a scale (doe-ray-
me-far-so). It "remembers" something of its history and thus is a little too
predictable for our tastes. Brown noises leave no expectation unfulfilled,
whereas white noises are devoid of any expectations that need to be ful-
filled. But midway between white and brown noise, when $a = 1$, lies the
special case of "$1/f$ noise." It is special because such signals possess "interesting" patterns over all time intervals.

In 1975, Richard Voss and John Clarke, two physicists at the University
of California at Berkeley, serendipitously discovered that human musical
compositions from a wide range of cultures have a spectrum that is very
closely approximated by $1/f$ noise over a wide range of frequencies (see
Figure 5.3).[16] Presumably, appealing music exhibits an optimal level of
novelty at the spectral level; it is neither too predictable like brown noise
nor randomly unpredictable like white noise. This may be telling us important things about the mind's first adaptations to the world of sound.
But if musical appreciation is a by-product of a more general pattern-pro-
cessing propensity of the brain, what sort of value are we perceiving in

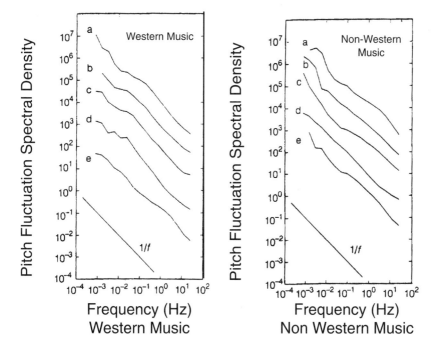

FIGURE 5.3   The Spectrum of Pitch variations versus Frequency found by Voss and Clark (see footnotes 16 and 18).

Notes: 1. Western traditions: a. medieval pre–fourteenth-century music; b. Beethoven; c. Debussy; d. Richard Strauss; e. the Beatles.
2. Non-Western traditions: a. *Ba*-Benzele Pygmies; b. classical Japanese; c. Indian ragas; d. Russian folk music; e. American rhythm and blues. All display a close affinity for the 1/f spectrum.

these sounds?; why are our senses especially aesthetically sensitive to 1/f noises?

It is significant that the world around us is full of variations with 1/f spectra. One reason is the prevalence of sequential processes in the natural world. Benoit Mandelbrot claimed that our nervous system acts as a spectral filter, preferentially passing 1/f noise to the brain whilst filtering out white noise at the periphery to prevent the brain from being swamped with uninteresting random background noise about the world.[17] An optimal response to signals with 1/f form might well be the best investment of resources that the system can make, or it may be the simplest signal for the nervous system to decode from vibrations in the inner ear.

It is also interesting that the 1/f spectrum is one that characterises processes like the sand pile, which display self-organising criticality. In a self-organised critical state, a system is optimally sensitive to influences: a single sand grain can produce an avalanche over the whole surface of the pile. Thus, perhaps, the critical state characterising the music that we like reflects the sensitivity to nuances of performance that create such new experiences when we hear the same piece performed on different occasions. Our liking for the 1/f spectral signature may be a reflection of this sensitivity to small nuances of composition and performance.

Music is the purest art form. Our minds receive a sequence of sounds woven into a pattern—undistracted by the other senses. The fact that a wide range of music exhibits a 1/f spectrum for its variations in loudness, pitch, and interval, across the whole range from classical to jazz and rock, suggests that this appeal arises from an affinity for the statistical features of natural noises whose detection and assimilation were adaptively advantageous to humans. This affinity extends to many varieties of non-Western music; there is a good approximation to 1/f noise in all of the cases studied: from Ba-Benzele Pygmies, traditional Japanese music, and Indian ragas to Russian folk songs and American blues (see Figure 5.3).[18]

A very interesting experiment would be to determine whether the spectrum of whale song is close to 1/f and to discover whether there are well-developed human musical traditions that do not display 1/f spectra. Modern atonal or "random" electronic music doesn't count, for obvious reasons.

One should not regard this argument as totally reductionist, any more than one should take seriously claims of music lovers that music is a transcendental form whose charms are beyond understanding and whose magic might disappear if too fully understood. We need not value art forms less for understanding their appeal. In any event, the power spectrum of music gives a far from complete measure of its structure. If a musical composition were played backwards, it would still have a 1/f spectrum, but it might well be unappealing to the ear. Our minds, with their propensity to analyse, distinguish, and respond to sounds of certain sorts yet ignore others, have evolutionary histories. Musicality seems most reasonably explained as an elaboration of abilities and susceptibilities that were evolved originally for other, more mundane but vital purposes. Our aptitude for sound processing converged upon a sensitivity for certain sound patterns because their recognition optimised the reception of vital information.

Musical appreciation is a by-product of this complex process. With the emergence of a more elaborate processing ability that we call consciousness has come the ability to explore and exploit our innate sensibility to sound, leading in turn to the creation of organised forms of sound that explore the whole range of pitches and intensities to which the human ear is sensitive. Those forms diverge in their stylistic nuances, as do the decorations around people's necks and in their homes, from culture to culture. But the universality of musical appreciation and the common spectral character of so much of the sound that we embrace behooves us to look for the universal aspects of early experience for an explanation. Had the sounds that fill our world been different in their spectral properties, we would have developed a penchant for sound with quite different structures—structures that from one perspective would have been more surprising or more predictable.

Alternatively, the source of 1/f noise in our environment may be a consequence of statistical processes of such generality that this form of noise would be ubiquitous in almost any naturally arising environment—terrestrial or extraterrestrial. Our ears may be optimised to be sensitive to sound sequences with a 1/f spectral signature because they are most likely to contain nonrandom information about the environment, which aids survival. Hence, sensitivity to 1/f sounds could be adaptive, and our appreciation for music of that spectral form is a by-product of adaptation. If so, we might have been overly pessimistic in believing that music could not be used to communicate with extraterrestrials. If, as we might expect, their environments display many 1/f spectral variations, they should have evolved a special sensitivity to them. When transformed into the appropriate medium, they might well appreciate some of our music. Which is just as well because the Voyager spacecraft, launched in 1977 and now heading for the stars, contains an elaborate recording of terrestrial sounds. Ninety minutes of music were included—Bach, Beethoven, rock and jazz, together with folk music from a variety of countries. The senders didn't know it, but it all has a 1/f spectrum.

Notes

1. J. D. Barrow, *The World Within the World* (Oxford: Oxford University Press, 1988).

2. G. Chaitin, "Randomness and Mathematical Proof," *Scientific American* (May 1975), pp. 47–52.

3. J. D. Barrow, *Theories of Everything: The Quest for the Ultimate Explanation* (Oxford: Oxford University Press, 1991; London: Vintage, 1992).

4. G. Chaitin, *Algorithmic Information Theory* (Cambridge: Cambridge University Press, 1987).

5. M. Green, "Superstrings," *Scientific American* (September 1986), p. 48; D. Bailin, "Why Superstrings," *Contemporary Physics* 30 (1989), p. 237; P. C. W.

Davies and J. R. Brown, eds., *Superstrings: A Theory of Everything* (Cambridge: Cambridge University Press, 1988).

6. H. Pagels, *Perfect Symmetry* (London: Michael Joseph, 1985); A. Zee, *Fearful Symmetry: The Search for Beauty in Modern Physics* (London: Macmillan, 1986); S. Weinberg, *The Discovery of Sub-atomic Particles* (New York: W. H. Freeman, 1983).

7. M. Green, J. Schwarz, and E. Witten, *Superstring Theory*, 2 vols. (Cambridge: Cambridge University Press, 1987).

8. Barrow, *Theories of Everything*; Davies and Brown, *Superstrings*.

9. J. D. Barrow, *Pi in the Sky: Counting, Thinking and Being* (Oxford: Oxford University Press, 1992); H. Moravec, *Mind Children* (Cambridge, Mass.: Harvard University Press, 1988).

10. J. Gleick, *Chaos: Making a New Science* (London: Viking, 1987); I. Stewart, *Does God Play Dice? The Mathematics of Chaos* (Oxford: Blackwells, 1989).

11. C. Gough, "Challenges of High T_c," *Physics World* (December 1991), p. 26.

12. S. Lloyd and H. Pagels, "Complexity and Thermodynamics Depth," *Annals of Physics* (New York, 1988), pp. 186, 188.

13. P. C. W. Davies, *The Cosmic Blueprint* (Oxford: Heinemann, 1987).

14. P. Bak, C. Tang, and K. Wiesenfeld, "Self-organising Criticality," *Physics Review* A38, p. 364; P. Bak, "Self-organising Criticality," *Scientific American* (January 1991), pp. 46–53.

15. J. D. Barrow, *The Artful Universe* (Oxford and New York: Oxford University Press, 1995).

16. R. Voss and J. Clarke, "1/f Noise in Music and Speech," *Nature* 278 (1975), p. 317; Voss and Clarke, "1/f Noise in Music: Music from 1/f Noise," *Journal of the Acoustical Society of America* 63 (1978), p. 258.

17. B. Mandelbrot, *The Fractal Geometry of Nature* (New York: W. H. Freeman, 1982).

18. R. Voss, "1/f (flicker) Noise: A Brief Review," *Proceedings of the 33rd Annual Symposium on Frequency Control* (Atlantic City: U.S. Army Electronics Research and Development Command, 1978), pp. 40–46.

6

Faith in the Truth

Daniel C. Dennett

Mathematics is the only religion that can prove it is a religion.
—John D. Barrow[1]

Is Science a Religion?

Is mathematics a religion at all? Is science? One often hears these days that science is "just" another religion. There are some interesting similarities. Established science, like established religion, has its bureaucracies and hierarchies of officials, its lavish and arcane installations of no utility apparent to outsiders, its initiation ceremonies. Like a religion bent on enlarging its congregation, it has a huge phalanx of proselytizers—who call themselves not missionaries but educators.

An amusing fantasy: an ill-informed observer witnesses the intricate, formal teamwork that goes into preparing a person for the arcane paraphernalia of positron emission tomography—a PET scan—and decides it must be a religious ceremony, a ritual sacrifice, perhaps, or the investiture of a new archbishop. But these are superficial appearances. What of the deeper similarities that have been proposed? Science, like religion, has its orthodoxies and heresies, doesn't it? Isn't the belief in the power of the scientific method a *creed*, on all fours with religious creeds in the sense that it is ultimately a matter of faith, no more capable of independent confirmation or rational support than any *other* religious creed? Notice that the question threatens to undermine itself: by contrasting faith with independent confirmation and rational support and denying that science as a whole can use its own methods to secure its own triumph, it pays homage to those very methods. There seems to be a curious asymmetry: scientists do not appeal to the authority of any religious leaders when their results are challenged, but many religions today would love to be able to secure the endorsement of science. A few have names that proclaim that desire: Christian Science and Scientology, for instance. We also have a word for science worship: "scientism." They are accused of scientism whose enthusiastic attitude towards the proclamations of science is all too similar to the attitudes of the devout: not cautious and objective but adoring, uncritical, or even fanatical.

If the scientists' *summum bonum,* or highest good, is truth, if scientists make truth their God, as some have claimed, is this not just as *parochial* an attitude as the worship of Jahweh, or Mohammed, or the Angel Moroni? No, our faith in the truth is, truly, *our* faith in the truth—a faith that is shared by all members of our species, even if there is great divergence in approved methods for obtaining it. The asymmetry noted above is real: faith in the truth has a priority claim that sets it apart from all other faiths.

The Priority of Truth

Right now, billions of organisms on this planet are engaged in a game of hide and seek, but it is not just a game for them. It is a matter of life and death. *Getting it right,* not making mistakes, has been of paramount importance to every living thing on this planet for more than 3 billion years, and so these organisms have evolved thousands of different ways of finding out about the world they live in, discriminating friends from foes and meals from mates, and ignoring the rest for the most part. It matters to them that they not be misinformed about these matters—indeed, nothing matters more—but they don't, as a rule, appreciate this fact. They are the beneficiaries of equipment exquisitely designed to get what matters right, but when their equipment malfunctions and gets matters wrong, they have no resources, as a rule, for noticing this, let alone deploring it. They soldier on, unwittingly. The difference between how things seem and how things really are is just as fatal a gap for them as it can be for us, but they are largely oblivious to it.

The *recognition* of the difference between appearance and reality is a human discovery. A few other species—some primates, some cetaceans, maybe even some birds—show signs of appreciating the phenomenon of "false belief"—*getting it wrong.* They exhibit sensitivity to the errors of others and perhaps even some sensitivity to their own errors as errors, but they lack the capacity for the reflection required to *dwell* on this possibility, and so they cannot use this sensitivity in the deliberate design of repairs or improvements of their own seeking gear or hiding gear. That sort of bridging of the gap between appearance and reality is a wrinkle that we human beings alone have mastered.

We are the species that discovered doubt. Is there enough food laid by for winter? Have I miscalculated? Is my mate cheating on me? Should we have moved south? Is it safe to enter this cave? Other creatures are often visibly agitated by their own uncertainties about just such questions, but because they cannot actually *ask themselves* these questions, they cannot articulate their predicaments for themselves or take steps to improve their grip on the truth. They are stuck in a world of appearances, making the best they can of how things seem and seldom, if ever, worrying about whether how things seem is how they truly are.[2]

We alone can be wracked with doubt, and we alone have been provoked by that epistemic itch to seek a remedy: better truth-seeking methods. Wanting to keep better track of our food supplies, our territories, our families, and our enemies, we discovered the benefits of talking it over with others, asking questions, and passing on lore. We invented culture. Then we invented measuring, arithmetic, maps, and writing. These communicative and recording innovations come with a built-in ideal: truth. The point of asking questions is to find *true* answers; the point of measuring is to measure *accurately*; the point of making maps is to *find* your way to your destination. There may be an Island of the Colour-blind (allowing Oliver Sacks his usual large dose of poetic license), but no Island of the People Who Do Not Recognize Their Own Children. The Land of the Liars could exist only in philosophers' puzzles; there are no traditions of False Calendar Systems for misrecording the passage of time. In short, the goal of truth goes without saying in every human culture.

Indeed, "saying" would not go at all without the ideal of truth. But no sooner had truth telling been invented than ways of exploiting this presumption were discovered as well: lying, mainly. As Talleyrand once cynically put it, language was invented so that we could conceal our thoughts from each other. Truth telling is, and must be, the background of all genuine communication, including lying. After all, deception only works when the would-be deceiver has a reputation for telling the truth.[3] Flattery would truly get you nowhere without the default presumption of truth telling: cooing like a dove or grunting like a pig would be as apt to curry favor.

The world of nonhuman animals has often discovered the possibility of false advertising. Where there are poisonous species that truly warn would-be predators of their danger with their bright colors, there are very often nonpoisonous species who mimic these bright colors, getting cheap protection thanks to a deceptive practice. But would-be liars among the animals have also discovered an enforcer of truth: the Zahavi principle. As the biologist Amotz Zahavi argued, only costly advertising wears its credibility on its sleeve because it can't be faked.[4] For instance, in the competition for mate choice, suitors with cumbersome antlers, peacock tails, or other handicaps are in effect saying: "I am so good that I can afford this huge cost and *still* survive." Competitors are forced to indulge in this extravagant outlay or go mateless. Nonhuman species, then, are often blindly guided down the straight and narrow path to veridicality; we alone among the animals appreciate truth "for its own sake." And—thanks to the science we have created in the pursuit of truth—we alone can also see why it is that truth, without being appreciated or even conceived of, is an ideal that constrains the perceptual and communicative activities of all animals.

We human beings use our communicative skills not just for truth telling but also for promise making, threatening, bargaining, storytelling, entertaining, mystifying, inducing hypnotic trances, and just plain kidding around. The prince of these activities is truth telling, however, and for this activity we have invented ever better tools. Alongside our tools for agriculture, building, warfare, and transportation, we have created a technology of truth: science.

Science as the Technology of Truth

Try to draw a straight line, or a circle, "freehand." Unless you have considerable artistic talent, the result will not be impressive. With a straight edge and a compass, on the other hand, you can practically eliminate the sources of human variability and get a nice, clean, objective result, the same every time.

Is the line really straight? How straight is it? In response to these questions, we develop ever finer tests, then tests of the accuracy of those tests, and so forth, bootstrapping our way to ever greater accuracy and objectivity. Scientists are just as vulnerable to wishful thinking, just as likely to be tempted by base motives, just as venal and gullible and forgetful as the rest of humankind. Scientists don't consider themselves to be saints; they don't even pretend to be priests (who, according to tradition, are supposed to do a better job than the rest of us at fighting off human temptation and frailty). Scientists take themselves to be just as weak and fallible as anybody else, but recognizing those very sources of error in themselves and in the groups to which they belong, they have devised elaborate systems to tie their own hands, forcibly preventing their frailties and prejudices from infecting their results.

It is not just the implements, the physical tools of the trade, that are designed to be resistant to human error. The organization of methods is also under severe selection pressure for improved reliability and objectivity. The classic example is the double-blind experiment, in which, for instance, neither the human subjects nor the experimenters themselves are permitted to know which subjects get the test drug and which the placebo, so that nobody's subliminal hankerings and hunches can influence the perception of the results. The statistical design of both individual experiments and suites of experiments is then embedded in the larger practice of routine attempts at replication by independent investigators, which is further embedded in a tradition—flawed, but recognized—of publication of both positive and negative results.

What inspires faith in arithmetic is the fact that hundreds of scribblers, working independently on the same problem, will all arrive at the same answer (except for those negligible few whose errors can be found and identified to the mutual satisfaction of all). This unrivaled objectivity is also found in geometry and the other branches of mathematics, which since antiquity have been the very model of certain knowledge set against the world of flux and controversy. In Plato's early dialogue, the *Meno*, Socrates and the slave boy work out together a special case of the Pythagorean theorem. Plato's example expresses the frank recognition of a standard of truth to be aspired to by all truth seekers, a standard that has not only never been seriously challenged but that has been tacitly accepted—indeed heavily relied upon, even in matters of life and death—by the most vigorous opponents of science. (Or do you know a church that keeps track of its flock, and their donations, without benefit of arithmetic?)

Yes, but science almost never looks as uncontroversial, as cut and dried, as arithmetic. Indeed, rival scientific factions often engage in propaganda battles as ferocious as anything to be found in politics or even in religious conflict. The fury with which the defenders of scientific orthodoxy often defend their doctrines against the heretics is probably unmatched in other arenas of human rhetorical combat. These competitions for allegiance—and, of course, funding—are designed to capture attention, and being well designed, they typically succeed. This has the side effect that the warfare on the cutting edge of any science draws attention away from the huge uncontested background, the dull metal heft of the axe that gives the cutting edge its power. What goes without saying, during these heated disagreements, is an organized, encyclopedic collection of agreed-upon, humdrum scientific fact.[5]

Robert Proctor usefully draws our attention to a distinction between neutrality and objectivity.[6] Geologists, he notes, know a lot more about oil-bearing shales than about other rocks—for the obvious economic and political reasons—but they do *know* objectively about oil-bearing shales. And much of what they learn about oil-bearing shales can be generalized to other, less favored rocks. We want science to be objective; we should not want science to be neutral. Biologists know a lot more about the fruit fly, *Drosophila*, than they do about other insects—not because you can get rich off fruit flies, but because you can get knowledge out of fruit flies easier than you can get it out of most other species. Biologists also know a lot more about mosquitoes than about other insects, and here it is because mosquitoes are more harmful to people than other species that might be much easier to study.

Many are the reasons for concentrating attention in science, and they all conspire to making the paths of investigation far from neutral; they do not, in general, make those paths any less objective. Sometimes, to be sure, one bias or another leads to a violation of the canons of scientific method. Studying the pattern of a disease in men, for instance, while neglecting to gather the data on the same disease in women, is not just not neutral; it is bad science, as indefensible in scientific terms as it is in political terms.

The methods of science aren't foolproof, but they are indefinitely perfectible. Just as important, there is a tradition of criticism that enforces improvement whenever and wherever flaws are discovered. The methods of science, like everything else under the sun, are themselves objects of scientific scrutiny, as *method* becomes *methodology*, the analysis of methods. Methodology in turn falls under the gaze of *epistemology*, the investigation of investigation itself—nothing is off limits to scientific questioning. The irony is that these fruits of scientific reflection, showing us the ineliminable smudges of imperfection, are sometimes used by those who are suspicious of science as their grounds for denying it a privileged status in the truth-seeking department—as if the institutions and practices they see competing with it were no worse off in these regards. But where are the examples of religious orthodoxy being simply abandoned in the face of irresistible evidence? Again and again in science, yesterday's heresies have become today's new orthodoxies. No religion exhibits that pattern in its history.

What difference in these institutions can explain this fact? It is, quite clearly, the leverage provided by the scientists' faith in the truth. Consider Richard Feynman's diagrams in quantum electrodynamics, for instance.[7] When I first encountered them, they seemed like numerology to me, ludicrously unlikely guides to truth, more like dealing Tarot cards or casting lots than science. It seemed strange that such a weird process would yield the truth—but it does work, and the reason it works can be understood (with effort!). And because it works and can be proven to work, yielding results of dazzling precision and accuracy, it has become an accepted part of orthodox scientific method. If casting lots or astrology could be demonstrated to yield results of similar accuracy, they too could be accommodated, along with the theory of why they worked, in orthodox science. But, of course, no such methods have ever been vindicated. Scientists have faith in the truth, but it is not blind faith. It is not like the faith that parents may have in the honesty of their children or that sports fans may have in the capacity of their heroes to make the winning plays. It is rather like the faith anybody can have in a result that has been independently arrived at by ten different teams.

Epistemology: Trying to Tell the Truth About Truth

The ultimate reflexive investigation of investigation occurs in that branch of philosophy known as epistemology, the theory of knowledge. Here too, controversies at the cutting edge have created a scale effect, a distortion that has often led to misinterpretations. Agreeing that truth is a very important concept, epistemologists have tried to say just *what truth is*—without going overboard. Just figuring out what is true about truth turns out to be a difficult task, however, a *technically* difficult task, in which definitions and theories that seem at first to be innocent lead to complications that soon entangle the theorist in dubious doctrines. Our esteemed and familiar friend, truth, tends to turn into Truth—with a capital T—an inflated concept of truth that cannot really be defended.

Here is just one of the paths that leads to difficulty: suppose knowledge consists of nothing but true propositions believed with justification, and then suppose that true propositions, unlike false propositions, express facts. What are facts? How many facts are there? (Tom, Dick, and Harry are sitting in a room. There's one fact. In addition to Tom, Dick, and Harry, the room they are sitting in, and whatever they are sitting on, we seem to have a plethora of other facts: Dick is not standing; there is no horse on which Tom is riding; and so forth, ad infinitum. Do we really need to countenance an infinity of further facts alongside the rather minimal furnishings of this little world?) Were there facts before there were fact finders, or are they rather like true sentences (of English, French, Latin, etc.), whose existence had to await the creation of human languages? Are facts independent of the minds of those who believe the propositions that express them? Do truths *correspond* to facts? What do the truths of mathematics correspond to, if anything? The categories begin to multiply, and no unified, obvious, agreed-upon story about truth emerges.[8] Skeptics, seeing apparent pitfalls in any absolute or transcendental version of truth, argue for milder versions, and their opponents argue back, showing the flaws in the rival attempts at theory. Unremitting controversy reigns.

This modest but intermittently brilliant investigation of the very meaning of the word "truth" has had some mischievous consequences. Some have thought that the philosophical arguments showing the hopelessness of the inflated doctrines of truth actually showed that truth itself was nothing estimable or achievable after all. "Give it up," they seem to be saying. "Truth is an unachievable and misguided ideal." Then those who have gone on searching for an acceptable, defensible doctrine of truth appear to be clinging to an outworn creed, avowing a religion that they cannot secure by the methods of science itself. Epistemology begins to look like a mug's game—but only because the observers are forgetting all the points about truth that both sides agree upon. The effects of this distorted vision can be unsettling.

When I was a young untenured professor of philosophy, I once received a visit from a colleague from the comparative literature department, an eminent and fashionable literary theorist, who wanted some help from me. I was flattered to be asked and did my best to oblige, but the drift of his questions about various philosophical topics was strangely perplexing to me. For quite a while we were getting nowhere, until finally he managed to make clear to me what he had come for. He wanted "an epistemology," he said. *An* epistemology. Every self-respecting literary theorist had to sport an epistemology that season, it seems, and without one he felt naked, so he had come to me for an epistemology to wear—it was the very next fashion, he was sure, and he wanted the dernier cri in epistemologies. It didn't matter to him that it be sound or defensible, or (as one might as well say) *true*; it just had to be new and different and stylish. Accessorize, my good fellow, or be overlooked at the party.

At that moment, I perceived a gulf between us that I had only dimly seen before. It struck me at first as simply the gulf between being serious and being frivolous. But that initial surge of self-righteousness on my part was, in fact, a naive reaction. My sense of outrage, my sense that my time had been wasted by this man's bizarre project, was in its own way as unsophisticated as the reaction of the first-time theatergoer who leaps on the stage to protect the heroine from the villain. "Don't you understand?" we ask incredulously. "It's *make believe*. It's *art*. It isn't *supposed* to be taken literally!" Put in that context, perhaps this man's quest was not so disreputable after all. I would not have been offended, would I, if a colleague in the drama department had come by and asked if he could borrow a few yards of my books to put on the shelves of the set for his production of Tom Stoppard's play *Jumpers*. What, if anything, would be wrong in outfitting this fellow with a snazzy set of outrageous epistemological doctrines with which he could titillate or confound his colleagues?

What would be wrong would be that since this man didn't acknowledge the gulf, didn't even recognize that it existed, my acquiescence in his shopping spree would have contributed to the debasement of a precious commodity, the erosion of a valuable distinction. Many people, including both onlookers and participants, don't see this gulf or actively deny its existence, and therein lies the problem. The sad fact is that in some intellectual circles, inhabited by some of our more advanced thinkers in the arts and humanities, this attitude passes as a sophisticated appreciation of the futility of proof and the relativity of all knowledge claims. In fact, this opinion, far from being sophisticated, is the height of sheltered naïveté, made possible only by flatfooted ignorance of the proven methods of scientific truth seeking and their power. Like many another naïf, these thinkers, reflecting on the manifest inability of *their* methods of truth seeking to achieve stable and valuable results, innocently generalize from their own cases and conclude that nobody else knows how to discover the truth either.

Among those who contribute to this problem, I am sorry to say, is an earlier Amnesty Lecturer in Oxford, my good friend Dick Rorty.[9] Richard Rorty and I have been constructively disagreeing with each other for over a quarter of a century now. Each of us has taught the other a great deal, I believe, in the reciprocal process of chipping away at our residual points of disagreement. I can't name a living philosopher from whom I have learned more. Rorty has opened up the horizons of contemporary philosophy, shrewdly showing us philosophers many things about how our own projects have grown out of the philosophical projects of the distant and recent past, while boldly describing and prescribing future paths for us to take. But there is one point over which he and I do not agree at all—not yet—and that concerns his attempt over the years to show that philosophers' debates about Truth and Reality really do erase the gulf, really do license a slide into some form of relativism. In the end, Rorty tells us, it is all just "conversations," and there are only political or historical or aesthetic grounds for taking one role or another in an ongoing conversation.

Rorty has often tried to enlist me in his campaign, declaring that he could find in my own work one explosive insight or another that would help him with his project of destroying the illusory edifice of objectivity. One of his favorite passages is the one with which I ended my book *Consciousness Explained*:

> It's just a war of metaphors, you say—but metaphors are not "just" metaphors; metaphors are the tools of thought. No one can think about consciousness without them, so it is important to equip yourself with the best set of tools available. Look what we have built with our tools. Could you have imagined it without them?[10]

"I wish," Rorty says, "he had taken one step further, and had added that such tools are all that inquiry can ever provide, because inquiry is never 'pure' in the sense of [Bernard] Williams' 'project of pure inquiry.' It is always a matter of getting us something we want."[11] But I would never take that step, for although metaphors are indeed irreplaceable tools of thought, they are not the only such tools. Microscopes and mathematics and magnetic resonance imaging (MRI) scanners are among the others. Yes, any inquiry is a matter of getting us something we want: the truth about something that matters to us, if all goes as it should.

When philosophers argue about truth, they are arguing about how not to inflate the truth about truth into the Truth about Truth, some absolutist doctrine that makes indefensible demands on our systems of thought. Their arguments are, in this regard, similar to debates about, say, the reality of time or the reality of the past. There are some deep, sophisticated, worthy philosophical investigations into whether, properly speaking, the past is real. Opinion is divided, but you entirely misunderstand the point of these disagreements if you suppose that they undercut claims such as the following:

> Life first emerged on this planet more than three thousand million years ago.
>   The Holocaust happened during World War II.
>   Jack Ruby shot and killed Lee Harvey Oswald at 11:21 A.M., Dallas time, November 24, 1963.

These are truths about events that really happened. Their denials are falsehoods. No sane philosopher has ever thought otherwise, though in the heat of battle, they have sometimes made claims that could be so interpreted.

Richard Rorty deserves his large and enthralled readership in the arts and humanities and in the "humanistic" social sciences, but when his readers enthusiastically interpret him as encouraging their postmodernist skepticism about truth, they trundle down paths he himself has refrained from traveling. When I press him on these points, he concedes that there is indeed a useful concept of truth that survives intact after all the corrosive philosophical objections have been duly entered. This serviceable, modest concept of truth, Rorty acknowledges, has its uses: when we want to compare two maps of the countryside for reliability, for instance, or when the issue is whether the accused did or did not commit the crime as charged.

Even Richard Rorty, then, acknowledges the gap, and the importance of the gap, between appearance and reality, between those theatrical exercises that may entertain us without pretence of truth telling and those that aim for and often hit the truth. He calls it a "vegetarian" concept of truth. Very well, then, let's all be vegetarians about the truth. Scientists never wanted to go the whole hog anyway.

The Truth Can Hurt

Everybody wants the truth. If you wonder whether your neighbor has cheated you, if there are any fish in this part of the lake, or which way to walk to get home, you are interested in truth. Why, though, if truth is so wonderful and so obtainable, is there so much antagonism towards science? Everybody appreciates truth; not everybody appreciates the truth-finding tools of science.

Some, it seems, would prefer other, more traditional methods of getting at the truth: astrology, divination, the use of soothsayers and gurus and shamans, trance channeling, and consultation of a variety of holy texts. Here the verdict of science is so familiar that I hardly need repeat it: as entertainment or stretching exercises for the mind, these various activities have their merits, but as truth-seeking methods, none can compete with science, a fact regularly conceded, tacitly, by those who defend their favorite alternative practice by citing what they claim to be *scientific support*—what else?—of its claims to power. One never encounters a believer in trance channeling enlisting the support of an association of astrologers or a college of cardinals, but every shred of putative statistical evidence, every stray physicist or mathematician who can be found to offer friendly testimony, is eagerly brandished.

Why, then, if science is regularly appealed to even by those who seek to spread the word about alternatives, is there also so much dread? The answer is well known: the truth can hurt. Indeed it can. That is no illusion, but it is sometimes denied or ignored by scientists and others who pretend to believe that *truth above all* is the highest good. Surely it is not. I can easily describe circumstances in which I myself would lie or suppress the truth in order to prevent some human suffering. An old woman at the end of her days, living her life vicariously through tales of the heroic achievements of her son—are you going to tell her when he is arrested, convicted of some terrible crime, and humiliated? Isn't it better for her to leave this world in ignorant bliss? Of course it is, say I. But note that even here, we have to understand these cases as exceptions to the rule. We couldn't give this woman the comfort of our lies if lies were the general rule; she has to believe us when we talk to her.

It is a fact that people often don't want to know the truth. It is a more unsettling fact that people often don't want *other* people to know the truth. It darkens counsel to attempt to transform these facts into support for the fatuous idea that faith in the truth is itself a culture-bound, parochial, or in any way optional human attitude. The father of the accused who sits listening in court to the testimony, the woman who wonders if her husband is cheating on her—they may well not want to know the truth, and they may be right not to want to know the truth, but they believe in the truth. Very clearly they do; they know that the truth is there to be shunned or embraced, and that it matters. That's *why* they may well not want to know the truth—because the truth can hurt. They may manage to deceive themselves into thinking that their attitude towards the truth on this occasion reflects ill on truth and on the very processes of truth finding and truth seeking, but if so, this really is self-deception. The most they can hope to cling to is that there may be good reasons, the best of reasons—in the court of truth, note—for sometimes suppressing or ignoring the truth.

Should we not, then, consider suppressing the truth on a large scale, protecting various threatened groups from its corrosive effects? Consider what inevitably happens when our scientific culture and its technology are introduced to populations that have hitherto been spared its innovations. What effects will cellular telephones and MTV and high-tech weaponry (and the high-tech medicine to deal with the effects of the high-tech weaponry) have on the underdeveloped peoples of the Third World? Many destructive and painful effects, no doubt. But we don't have to look at electronic wizardry to see the damage that can be done. Tijs Goldschmidt, in his fascinating book *Darwin's Dreampond*, tells of the devastating effects of introducing the Nile perch into Lake Victoria: the amazing species flock of cichlid fish was nearly extinguished in a few years, a catastrophic loss—for biologists, but not necessarily for the people who lived on its shores and who now could supplement their subsistence diet with the bounties of a new fishery.[12] Goldschmidt also tells, however, of a similar cultural effect: the extinction of traditional Sukuma baskets.

> These watertight baskets were woven by women and used at celebrations as vessels for consuming vast quantities of *pombe*, a millet beer. . . . Blades of grass dyed with manganese were woven into the baskets in geometric patterns with a symbolic significance. It wasn't always possible to find out what the patterns meant because the arrival of the *mazabethi*—the aluminum dishes named after Queen Elizabeth that had been introduced on a large scale under British rule—had signified the end of the *masonzo* culture. I spoke to an old woman in a little village who, after more than thirty years, was still incensed about the mazabethi. . . . "*Sisi wanawake*, we women, we used to weave baskets while sitting around and chatting with each other. I don't see anything wrong with that. Each woman did her best to make the most beautiful basket possible. The mazabethi put an end to all that."[13]

Even more sad, I think, is the effect reported by Katharine Milton of the introduction of steel axes to the Panare Indians of Venezuela.

> In the past, when stone axes were used, various individuals came together and worked communally to fell trees for a new garden. With the introduction of the steel ax, however, one man can clear a garden by himself . . . collaboration is no longer mandatory *nor particularly frequent*.[14]

These people lose what Milton calls their traditional "web of cooperative interdependence," and they also lose a great deal of the knowledge they have amassed over centuries of the fauna and flora of their own world. Often their very languages are extinguished in a generation or two. These are great losses, without any doubt. But what policies should we adopt regarding them?

First, we should take note of the obvious: when traditional cultures encounter Western culture, the traditionalists enthusiastically adopt almost all the new practices, the new tools, the new ways. Why? Because they know what they have always desired, valued, and wished for, and they find that these novelties are better means to their own ends than their old ways. Steel axes replace stone axes, outboard motors replace sails, modern medicine replaces witch doctoring, and transistor radios and cellular phones are eagerly sought. These people turn out to be no better than we are at foreseeing the long-term effects of their choices, but on the basis of the information they consider, they choose rationally.

Yes, there are times, to be sure, when their innocence is taken advantage of by meretricious "advertising" cunningly aimed at their sheltered appreciation of the possibilities life has in store. But notice that this deplorable tactic is not the special province of those who would exploit them. Those who would protect them from modern technology are apparently prepared to grit their teeth and lie to them on a large scale: "Conceal your high-tech wonders from them! If you must give them something, palm off some shiny beads, or other tidbits that they can readily incorporate into their traditional culture."

Is this any way to treat adult members of our species? Do we not all have, among our human rights, the right to know the truth? It is shockingly paternalistic to say that we should shield these people from the fruits of civilization. What, are they like elephants, to be put in a preserve? I recommend that we treat them as we treat our own citizens: we offer them all the truth-seeking tools in our kit, so that they can make an informed choice—if they so choose. To be sure, that course of action is a one-way street. Once they have been so informed, we have already violated their pristine purity. There's no going back.

You can't have it both ways. If these are human adults, then they have a right to know, do they not? Would you really advocate taking steps to prevent them from educating themselves? Educating themselves will turn them into something radically different; they will lose many of their old ways. Some of this will be good riddance, and some, no doubt, will be tragic. But what standard would you use to anchor the "right" ways for them? The ways of the last hundred years, or of last ten years, or of the last ten millennia? And more pressing, what would give us the right in the first place to treat them differently from the way we treat our own citizens?

Who cries out for this self-imposed restraint, by the way? Who beseeches us to button our "imperialist" lips and keep our so-called scientific truths to ourselves? Not, typically, the people, but rather their self-declared spiritual leaders. It is they, not their flocks, who demand that their flocks be shielded from the corrosive and irreversible influences of our scientific culture of truth. Those people who work in "cultural studies" and others who fly the banner of multiculturalism should linger thoughtfully over the following suggestion: their well-meaning policy of tolerance for traditional policies that deny free access to the truth-seeking tools of science is often—more often than not, I would judge—a policy in the service of tyrants.

In Western culture, the idea of informed consent is one of the cornerstones of liberty. In other cultures, the very idea of informing the people so that they might consent or not is viewed with hostility. The next century will, I hope, sweep away this hostility. Indeed, I think it will become more and more impractical for political leaders to preserve the uninformedness of their people. All we need do is just keep putting out the word, clearly and with scrupulous concern for telling the truth. There is really nothing new in this suggestion. Institutions such as the BBC World Service have been doing just that, with tremendous success, for decades. And year after year, the elite in every nation in the world send their children to our universities for their education. They know, perhaps better than we ourselves appreciate, that the science and technology of truth seeking is our most valuable export.

Notes

1. John D. Barrow, *The World Within the World* (Oxford: Oxford University Press, 1988) p. 257.

2. The world of appearances for each of them has been vigorously biased by natural selection in the direction of their narrow best interests. Which facts do they find? Their sense organs—and their information-gathering behaviors using these sense organs—have been tuned to "narcissism" designed to exaggerate, smear, discount, and in other ways adjust or edit their gifts of meaning in favor of life-preserving interpretations (see Kathleen Akin, "Science and Our Inner Lives," in Marc Berkoff and Dale Jamieson, eds., *Interpretation and Explanation in the Study of Animal Behavior*, vol. 1 [Boulder, Colo.: Westview Press, 1990], pp. 414–427). This does not prevent them from tracking facts. Rather, it determines that the facts they track are those with a built-in perspective. Thus, they do not register "here is water" in the chemist's sense but in the thirsty organism's sense that glosses over the niceties of definition and ignores impurities up to the point at which they become a health issue. Exactitude of definition or the "transduction" of a "natural kind" has never been one of nature's goals. Failure to appreciate this point has led to a cottage industry of philosophical fantasy (about Twin Earth, XYZ, and other chimeras).

3. Richard Dawkins and John Krebs opened up the field of theoretical investigation of this side of communication; see "Animal Signals: Information or Manip-

ulation," in J. R. Krebs and N. B. Davies, eds., *Behavioral Ecology* (Oxford: Blackwell Scientific Publications, 1978), pp. 282–309. See Marc Hauser, *The Evolution of Communication* (Cambridge, Mass.: MIT Press, 1996) for a masterful overview of the empirical and theoretical work in the field.

4. The "Zahavi principle" was first outlined in Amotz Zahavi, "Mate Selection—a Selection for a Handicap," *Journal of Theoretical Biology* 53 (1975), pp. 205–214.—*Ed.*

5. Even supposedly trained observers—such as those working in the new fields of "science studies" or the sociology of science—often overlook this mountain of quiet results, concentrating their attention on the noisy and exciting moments. In anthropology generally, this is a well-recognized problem of observer bias. Consider: you have obtained a grant to study some relatively exotic human group, and you spend several years far from home, enduring hardships, tedium, and isolation. You would surely find it extremely hard to contemplate the prospect of coming back with the following discovery: they're pretty much just like us. Or worse: they actually do just what they say they do. Why worse? Because if you, the anthropologist, can't offer an account that contradicts or otherwise improves on the account we already have from their own mouths, it seems you have been wasting your time—and our grant money. There is, then, a natural, even reasonable, human bias in favor of concentrating on the extraordinary, in hopes of finding something riveting, something new, something surprising to repay the effort of the investigation.

6. See, in particular, Robert N. Proctor, *Value-free Science? Purity and Power in Modern Knowledge* (Cambridge, Mass.: Harvard University Press, 1991).—*Ed.*

7. The classic explanation is Richard Feynman, *QED: The Strange Theory of Light and Matter* (Princeton: Princeton University Press, 1985).

8. If you think, impatiently, that there is an obvious way of cutting through this Gordian knot, wonderful. Write up your solution and submit it to a philosophy journal. If you're right, you'll become famous for solving problems that have stymied the cleverest epistemologists for years, if not centuries. But be forewarned: it was just such brave convictions that led most of us into this discipline.

9. See Richard Rorty, "Human Rights, Rationality, and Sentimentality," in Stephen Shute and Susan Hurley, eds., *On Human Rights: Oxford Amnesty Lectures 1993* (New York: Basic Books, 1993), pp. 112–134.—*Ed.*

10. Daniel C. Dennett, *Consciousness Explained* (New York and Boston: Little, Brown, 1991), p. 455.

11. Richard Rorty, "Holism, Intrinsicality, and the Ambition of Transcendence," in Bo Dahlbom, ed., *Dennett and His Critics* (Oxford: Blackwell, 1993), p. 198.

12. A species flock is a group of species descending from a common ancestor and originating within a defined area. See the definition given by Tijs Goldschmidt, in the glossary appended to his book *Darwin's Dreampond.*

13. Tijs Goldschmidt, *Darwin's Dreampond* (Cambridge, Mass.: MIT Press, 1996), p. 39.

14. Katharine Milton, "Civilization and Its Discontents," *Natural History* (March 1992), pp. 37–42 (emphasis added).

7

The Myths We Live By

Mary Midgley

Neutral or Not?

People answer questions about the values of science in two quite distinct
ways today. On the one hand, science is often praised for being value-
free—objective, unbiased, neutral, a pure source of facts. Just as often,
however, science is spoken of as being itself a source of values, perhaps
indeed the only true source of them. For example, the great evolutionist
Conrad Waddington wrote in 1941: "Science by itself is able to provide
mankind with a way of life which is . . . self-consistent and harmonious. . . . So far as I can see, the scientific attitude of mind is *the only one*
which is, at the present day, adequate to do this" (emphases mine).[1] As
we shall see, too, many serious theorists have claimed that science is
"omnicompetent"—that is, able to answer every kind of question.

Where we meet such clashes, the truth is usually somewhere in the
middle and more complicated than it looks. The word *science* is surely being used with a different meaning in these two claims. We do indeed
sometimes think of science as simply an immense store of objective facts,
unquestionable facts about such things as measurements, temperatures,
and chemical composition. But a store cupboard is, in itself, not very exciting. What makes science into something much grander and more interesting than this is the huge, ever-changing imaginative structure of
ideas by which scientists contrive to connect and understand the facts.
The general concepts, metaphors, and images which make up this structure cannot possibly be objective and antiseptic in this same way. They
grow out of images drawn from everyday life because that's the only
place to get them. They relate theory to that everyday life and are meant
to influence it. As history shows, these concepts and images change as
the way of life around them changes. And after they have been used in

science, they are often reflected back into that everyday life in altered forms, apparently charged with a new scientific authority.

I will discuss later several very potent ideas that have moved in this way from ordinary thought to affect the course of science and have then returned to outside usage reshaped by scientific use. Right away, one might name the concept of a *machine*, of a *self-interested* individual, and of *competition* between such individuals. Metaphorical concepts like these are quite properly used by scientists, but they are not just passive pieces of apparatus like thermostats. They have their own influence. They are parts of powerful myths.

By myths I do not, of course, mean lies. I mean the imaginative patterns that we all take for granted—the ongoing dramas inside which we seem to live. These patterns shape the mental maps that we refer to when we want to place something. Such patterns are not just a distraction from real thought, as positivists have suggested. Nor are they a disease. They are the matrix of thought, the mental contours that shape it. They determine our selection of topics; they decide what we think important and what we ignore. They provide the channels that we vitally need if we are to organise the mass of incoming data that we have to deal with.

They can, however, of course, also affect our beliefs by distorting our selection and slanting our thinking. That is why we need to watch them carefully. This is specially urgent in times of rapid change because patterns of thought that are really useful in one age can make serious trouble in the next one. These patterns don't then necessarily have to be dropped, but they do often have to be reshaped or balanced by other thought-patterns in order to correct their faults.

When we think about these changes, it is important to notice that myths do not alter in the rather brisk, wholesale way that much contemporary imagery suggests. The belief in instant ideological change is itself a favorite myth of the recent epoch that we are now beginning to abuse as *modern*. Descartes may have started it when he launched his still-popular town-planning metaphor, comparing the whole of current thought to an unsatisfactory city which should be knocked down and replaced by a better one.[2] Today, too, another influential image, drawn from Nietzsche, works on the model of the "Deaths" column in a newspaper. Here you just report the death of something—Art, or Poetry, or History, or the Author, or God, or Nature, or Metaphysics, or whatever—publish its obituary, and then forget about it.

The trouble with images like these is that such large-scale items don't suddenly vanish. Prominent ideas cannot die until the problems that arise within them have been resolved. They are not just a kind of external parasite. They are not alien organisms—"memes" that happen to have infested us and can be cleared away with the right insecticide. They are organic parts of our lives, elements in our thinking. So they follow conservation laws within it. Instead of dying, they transform themselves gradually into something different, something that is often hard to recognise and to understand. The Marxist pattern of complete final revolution is not at all appropriate here. We do better to talk organically of our life as an ecosystem trying painfully to adapt itself to changes in the world around it.

In this lecture I want to concentrate on certain particular myths that have come down to us from the Enlightenment and are now giving trouble. Enlightenment concepts tend to be extremely simple and sweeping. Dramatic simplicity has been one of their chief attractions and is also their chronic weakness, especially when they need to be applied in detail. For instance, the Enlightenment's overriding emphasis on freedom often conflicts with other equally important ideals such as justice or compassion. Complete commercial freedom, for example, or complete freedom to carry weapons, can lead to serious harm and injustice. We need, then, to supplement the original dazzling insight about freedom with a more discriminating priority system. And again, the insistence on individuality which has so enriched our lives degenerates, if we don't watch it critically, into the kind of mindless competitive individualism that today impoverishes those same lives by locking people up in meaningless solitude.

In the case of the physical sciences, which are our present business, we already know that Enlightenment ideas have been much too simple and dramatic. For instance, they suggested that physics could expect to reveal a far simpler kind of order in the world than has turned out to be available. This simplification did, of course, play a great part in making possible the astonishing success of these sciences. It gave Western civilisation an understanding of natural "mechanisms" (as we call them) far beyond that of any other culture and a wealth of technology that other cultures had never dreamed of.

This tremendous achievement is quite rightly being celebrated by other contributors to this book, and of course I join in their celebration. But we, the heirs of this great intellectual empire, don't actually need to come together simply to praise it. We don't now need to tell each other that science is good any more than we need to say that freedom is good or democracy is good. As ideals, these things are established in our society. But when once ideals are established and are supposed to be working, we have to deal with the surprisingly complicated reality that is supposed to be expressing them. Today, some people plainly do *not* think that science is altogether good. At times there are similar doubts about democracy and freedom. When this sort of thing happens, those of us who care about the ideals need to ask what is going wrong with the way they are being incorporated in the world. We have to consider how best to understand the present condition of science, how best to live with its difficulties and responsibilities, and how to shape its further development so as to avoid these distortions.

Changing Scenes

In trying to do this, I want chiefly to discuss three current myths—the social contract myth, the progress myth, and the myth of omnicompetent science. These three myths are connected, not just because they all need rethinking but because the last of them impedes our efforts to deal with the first two and with many other problems as well. Exaggerated and distorted ideas about what science can do for us have led, during the nineteenth and twentieth centuries, to the rise of powerful, supposedly scientific ideologies. These ideologies (which I shall discuss) are actually not part of real science, but by claiming its authority they have blackened its name. I shall suggest that people who want, today, to defend science from attack need to take these parasites seriously and to go to some trouble to dissociate it from them. They also need to get rid of the absurd and embarrassing claim to "omnicompetence." Science, which has its own magnificent work to do, does not need to rush in and take over extraneous kinds of questions (historical, logical, ethical, linguistic, or the like) as well. The champions of physical science can be happy to see it as it is, as one great department of human thought among others, all of which cooperate in our efforts at understanding the world. This is a far more honorable status than that of a nineteenth-century political power trying to enlarge its empire by universal conquest.

The Expanding World

All three myths that I have mentioned belong to the Enlightenment. All of them still shape our intellectual and moral thinking. The world around us, however, has changed radically since the eighteenth century when these ideas were coined. Our drama—the play in which we are all acting—has shifted to an enormously larger theatre. We live now in a bigger world, bigger not just because the sheer number of humans has tripled in this century or because we are now better informed about them. An even more crucial change is the way in which our own power has increased. We urban humans have now become capable of doing serious harm all over the world, both to its human and its nonhuman inhabitants. This really is something new in human history. In fact, it is surely the biggest change our species has ever experienced—certainly the biggest since the invention of agriculture. No wonder if it throws us into culture shock and calls on us to alter some of our concepts.

At present, the problems that arise here about our duty to distant humans are often discussed separately from those about our misuse of other animals, and both are usually segregated from the environmental problems. Different academic departments and different political bodies commonly deal with these three matters. Feuds often arise among them. The division between the natural sciences and the humanities widens the split. But the link between them is crucial. The sudden enlargement of our power has transformed all these issues equally. In all these directions, technology has hugely multiplied both the range of matters that concern us and our ability to affect them. And though that ability often seems to be out of our hands as individuals, our civilisation as a whole clearly does bear some responsibility for producing this situation. Our trade, our investment, and our expressions of public opinion do indeed affect all sorts of distant events.

We find it hard to believe in this whole expansion. Can it really be true that we bear responsibility for things that happen to people and countries so far away from us? Can we even, still more oddly, have responsibilities towards the nonhuman world? Our current moral tradition makes it especially hard for us to grasp these things. It doesn't leave room for them. Yet the changes are real. They do demand some kind of adaptation from us, adaptation of a morality that was formed for a quite different, more manageable kind of world. We can't go on acting as if we were still in that world. On that path, there is no way through.

Human Rights and the Social Contract

This difficulty comes up strongly at present over the concept of universal human rights. That notion clashes with the Enlightenment idea that morality is essentially just a contract made between fellow citizens for civic purposes and ultimately for individual self-interest. Some political theorists, who are rather oddly known as realists, claim that we cannot have duties to people outside our own nation-state because they are not contractors in our society, and *rights* (they say) arise only from contract.[3] This is the idea that politicians are expressing when they reassure us that British interests must, of course, always come first.

The social contract myth is a typical piece of Enlightenment simplification. It was developed (quite properly) as an answer to the doctrine of the divine right of kings, a defence against the religious wars and oppressions that monarchs set going in the sixteenth and seventeenth centuries. It rested political authority on the consent of the governed, which is fine. But its limitation is that it leaves no room for duties to outsiders, thus bringing it into conflict with another equally central Enlightenment idea—namely, the unity of all humanity. *That* idea says that, if oppression is wrong, it is wrong everywhere, and that, therefore, anyone who can do something about it ought to do so. Quite early on, this wider concept was expressed by bold, noncontractual talk about the rights of man, which made possible widespread and effectual campaigns against things like slavery.

The clash between these two ideas is not a clash between different cultures but a clash between two closely related ideas within the same culture. It is not over yet because both these ideas are still crucial to us. They have both been parts of the same bold attempt to make human society more just and less brutal. They were both originally somewhat crude and have needed repeated adjustment. The idea of contract was the formal, legalistic, reductive side of this humanitarian campaign. The notion of universal rights expressed the outgoing, generous, sympathetic feeling that powered the campaign in the first place. The difficulty of reconciling these two elements has led to a lot of trouble. It has often been dramatised into a supposed irresolvable conflict between reason and feeling.

This is always a confused idea because all reasoning is powered by feeling, and all serious feeling has some reasoning as its skeleton. Thought and feeling are not opponents any more than shape and size. They are complementary aspects that appear on both sides of any argument.[4] Polarising these two as opposites is, however, always tempting, and on the issue of human rights it has been quite important that the reductive, contractual pattern was seen as the rational one and as being supported by physical science. The idea that people are solitary, self-contained, indeed selfish individuals who wouldn't be connected to their neighbours at all if they didn't happen to have made a contract looked rational because it reflected the atomic theory of the day, a theory which similarly reduced matter to hard, impenetrable, disconnected atoms like billiard balls. Each of these two images seemed to strengthen the other, and for some time each was seen, within its own sphere, as the only truly rational and scientific pattern of understanding. Social atomism, expressed as political and moral individualism, got quite undeserved support from the imagery used in science.

Today, of course, physics deals in particles of a very different kind, particles which are essentially fields, that is, patterns of connection. But on the human scene and in biology, a quite unrealistic social atomism is still alive and kicking and still thinks of itself as scientific. The kind of individualism that treats people, and indeed other organisms, as essentially separate, competitive entities, ignoring the fact that competition can't get going at all without an enormous amount of cooperation to make it possible, has been the dominant ideology of the last two decades. Today it is under attack, which results in a lot of controversy.

This debate has not been just a futile zero-sum game. On its good days it has been a creative tension, a fertile dialectic in which each element has helped the other to become more adequate and workable. An example of this occurred when Garret Hardin compared the position of privileged people today to a lifeboat, arguing fatalistically that once the boat was loaded, its passengers could do nothing to help those who were still in the water and ought not to try to.[5] Somebody replied that no doubt there was a lot in this, but the actual situation might be more like that on a damaged ocean liner, where the people in steerage report that the ship is sinking and the first-class passengers send back a message saying "Not at our end." This dialogue isn't the end of the debate, but it is surely a useful part of it. It brings out how odd it is to compare the genuinely helpless group in the lifeboat with the large, rich communities that still wield whatever power is available today in the world. These images do have something in common. In both, people confront the prospect of shipwreck, and in both there are real limits to what can be done. But the two positions have opposite practical implications.

Talk of human rights seems to express our current compromise between these two complementary insights. Most concerned people do, I suspect, now feel willing to use the words "human rights." In spite of the huge differences between various cultures, we believe that there are indeed some things that ought not to be done to anybody, anywhere. Whatever the doubts about rights, we can all recognise human wrongs.[6] So, anyone who can protest effectively against these things is in a position to do so, whatever culture they belong to. This kind of belief is not, I think, confined to the West. Oppressed people in all kinds of countries now appeal to it. And in general they don't seem to be using it merely as a foreign language but as a kind of intercultural lingua franca that everybody understands. In this way, it is possible to select the distant matters that really do call for our intervention, despite the gulfs that divide our societies.[7]

In this way we can bring the outgoing, generous element in Enlightenment thinking together with the narrowing, formal, legalistic side. In principle, and to some extent even in practice, we can combine the imperative force of the civic word *rights* with the universal scope of species-wide thinking. The work of reconciling these ideas still demands a good deal of hard ethical thinking (which is different from scientific thinking, though just as necessary), but for practical purposes the concept is usable. Amnesty International does make a difference to the world. I do not want to exaggerate here the extent to which this actually affects practice. Of course, that difference is miserably small. I am just pointing out that our official morality does have room for this extension. It does not force us to be fatalistic chauvinists, as it would if we were totally bound by contract thinking. We are not burdened, as we might have been, with the

kind of moral ideas that would completely paralyse our efforts to intervene. And if the nautical metaphor just mentioned is the right one—if
there really is just one ship and none of us can jump off it—this is surely
just as well.

It is interesting, by the way, to note how much difference our choice of
an image can make to our thinking on this topic. Imagery is never just
paint on the surface of ideas. It often determines their whole direction.

Going Beyond Humanity

So much, then, for distant humans. What about the claims of the environment? These ought to be obvious because it should be clear that, even if
we don't care directly about the wilderness itself, all humans do share a
common interest in preserving the biosphere they live on. But our culture
has found this kind of realisation surprisingly hard. Of course, this is
partly because the environmental alarm is more recent than the social
one. But, more deeply, it is also because this matter is much harder to
bring within the framework of contract. The idea of universal *human* fellow citizens is slightly more familiar. Various images of a worldwide su-
perstate or supercity already exist to relate it to civic thinking. The Stoics
talked of the World City, Cosmopolis, and St. Augustine talked of the
City of God. But nobody has yet made the Antarctic or the rain forest our
fellow citizens, and it is not easy to see how they could do so. These simply are not the kind of beings that live in cities or plead in law courts.
They don't make contracts. So, on the familiar model, it was hard to see
how they can have *rights*. And this does, apparently, make it hard for
some people to take our duties to them seriously.

In this matter, surely the perspective of the natural sciences can really
help us. For many scientists, love and reverence for the natural world
that they study has been a powerful motive, whereas in the humanistic
parts of Western culture, this love and reverence has been a good deal
less central. Indeed, humanism has often been deliberately exclusive. Enlightenment thinking often neglected nonhuman nature, especially since
the Industrial Revolution, though Jean-Jacques Rousseau did not, and
poets such as William Blake and William Wordsworth did what they
could to protest against the bias. That concentration on our own species
is what makes it so hard for us now to take in the facts of environmental
destruction or react to them effectively. We have taken the natural support system for granted.

Scientists who concern themselves with ecological matters can help us
enormously in this area. They do so even though, at present, they actually have difficulty doing it because this outgoing, reverent attitude to
nature became for a time rather unfashionable within science itself. It

was associated with "natural historians"—that is, with patient, wide-ranging observers like Darwin—rather than with the laboratory-based experts in microbiology who were for a time viewed as the only possible model of "the scientific." But this narrow perspective does seem to be shifting. The sociobiologist Edward Wilson celebrated "biophilia"—the love of all living things—as something absolutely central for science.[8] And again, James Lovelock's concept of Gaia, which expresses our proper reverence for our planet at the same time as suggesting scientific tools for diagnosing its troubles, is no longer viewed as something wild.[9] It is beginning to get the kind of serious attention within science that it deserves. In fact, the two aspects of science are beginning to come together again.

Should we say, then, that this love and reverence for nature is one of the *values of science*? If we are to talk about such values at all, it surely is. Perhaps, indeed, it is the only value that is in some sense peculiar to the natural sciences. The other values that we think of as scientific are the intellectual virtues such as honesty, disinterestedness, thoroughness, imaginative enterprise, and a devotion to truth. Those virtues are indeed scientific, but they are so in the older and wider sense of that word, which is by no means restricted to physical science. These values belong to every kind of disciplined and methodical thought. They belong to history and logic, to ethics and mathematics and linguistics and law, just as much as they do to the natural sciences. But those enquiries don't deal so directly with the nonhuman world around us, with the plants and animals and stars that we should surely honor and revere, as the natural sciences do. The love of living things—biophilia as Wilson calls it—has played a special part in the thought of many great scientists such as Darwin, and it is a vital element which their successors can bring to stir us up against our present dangers.

If we do manage to take up this wider perspective, it will, of course, make our moral position more complicated, not simpler. But this is bound to happen anyway. Already we have to arbitrate many conflicts between the interests of humans and nonhumans such as elephants or trees. People who do this on a simple contractual basis simply rule out the nonhuman party in advance. But that simple principle no longer convinces us, and we can't seriously go on using it. These clashes demand some sort of a compromise. Even in the short term, the interests of the two parties do not always conflict, and in the long term they often converge strongly. If the local people are forced to destroy the habitat, then they too will soon be destroyed, along with the trees and the elephants. This convergence is, of course, particularly obvious in the situations of indigenous peoples, who accordingly have often campaigned heroically to defend it.

Progress and Science

So far I have been discussing my first myth, that of the social contract. I have been suggesting that this sweeping, monolithic thought-pattern, used for quite good reasons by earlier thinkers in the Enlightenment, now hampers our thought. The narrow civic stereotype makes it hard for us to adapt to a changed world in which our increased power makes traditional social contract thinking disastrously parochial.

This is just one case, however, among many in which Enlightenment thinking, after its initial successes, becomes simplistic and procrustean. Often it seizes on a particular pattern of thought as the only one that can properly be called rational and extends it to quite unsuitable topics. This intellectual imperialism constantly favors the form over the substance of what is being said, the method over the aim of an activity, and precision of detail over completeness of cover. That formal bias is not, in fact, at all particularly rational, though it is often thought of as being so.

I have suggested that this simplistic habit is what people are usually complaining of today when they stigmatise recent thinking as *modern*. The actual word *modern* is pretty unsuitable here and surely cannot go on being used forever in this way to describe what is manifestly out-of-date. Besides, it is too vague.[10] We need clearer, more specific words for this fault, and for present purposes I suggest using ones like dogmatic, simplistic, and monolithic.

The same kind of trouble arises about my last two examples, the linked ideas of inevitable progress and the omnicompetence of science. Here certain ways of thinking which proved immensely successful in the early development of the physical sciences have been idealised, stereotyped, and treated as the only possible forms for rational thought across the whole range of our knowledge. As with the social contract, the trouble is not in the methods themselves, which are excellent in their own sphere. It lies in the sweeping nature of their application, the naïve academic imperialism that insists on exporting them to all sorts of other topics.

The myth of inevitable progress is one that has been around in a general form since the late eighteenth century. It arose then to express a new kind of confidence in man and the works of man, replacing the earlier Christian reliance on God and the afterlife. Today it is often linked with the idea of evolution, though this link belongs to Jean Baptiste Lamarck rather than to Darwin and has its roots in wish fulfilment or in religion, not in biology. That association has, however, probably helped to give the idea of progress a quite undeserved aura of scientific respectability. And it has also probably strengthened the idea that belief in progress required faith in the omnicompetence of science.

Since H. G. Wells's day, the future has been seen as a special kind of imaginary country, the country that we see on *Tomorrow's World*, a country dripping with all the latest science and technology.[11] At first, this future land was approached with euphoric confidence which was shown by odious talk about the need to "drag people kicking and screaming into the twentieth century." (Fortunately, we do not seem now to be talking in this way about the new millennium.) Later, of course, there was disillusion, which I consider presently. But before the disillusion set in, scientistic prophets proclaimed their total confidence in the omnicompetence of science.

That phrase is not just a satirical parody of their faith. It has been used, quite literally, by a number of influential theorists to claim that something called science could indeed encompass the whole range of human thought on all subjects. Auguste Comte, the founder of positivism, originally sketched out this claim, and the philosophers of the Vienna Circle crystallised it soon after the First World War. Thus Rudolf Carnap ruled, "When we say that scientific knowledge is unlimited, we mean that *there is no question whose answer is in principle unattainable by science*" (Carnap's emphasis).[12] This extraordinary claim is still supported by some contemporary writers such as Peter Atkins, though of course many scientists today have not the slightest wish to make it.[13]

More importantly, the claim has been very influential in the outside world—so much so that it is not surprising if people now react against it. Many lay people, including some in high places, have declared a comprehensive, all-purpose faith in science. Thus Pandit Nehru, addressing the National Institute of Science of India in 1960, observed:

> It is science *alone* that can solve the problems of hunger and poverty, of insanitation and illiteracy, of superstition and deadening custom and tradition, of vast resources running to waste, of a rich country inhabited by starving people. . . . The future belongs to science and to those who make friends with science.[14] (my emphasis)

The interesting thing here is not just Nehru's confidence but what he meant by science—a point that I mentioned at the outset and that now becomes central. He clearly did *not* mean just a memory bank, a store of information. He meant a whole new ideology, a moral approach that would justify using those facts to revolutionise society. And during much of the twentieth century, the word *scientific* has constantly been used in this value-laden sense. Often it has not stood for any particular form of scientific knowledge but for a new scale of values, a new priority system. People like B. F. Skinner, who claimed that "we live in a scientific age," did not just mean an age which used science. They meant an age that is *guided* by science—an age which, in some way, chooses its ideals as well as its medicines and its breakfast foods on grounds provided by scientific research. This new system was certainly not seen as value free but as a moral signpost that could take the place of religion.

Science Alone?

Nehru and Waddington and Carnap spoke here for a whole mass of their contemporaries for whom science meant a great deal more than simply correct information. Information in itself can (no doubt) be said to be "value free," but this is because information on its own is valueless. It only begins to have a value when it becomes capable of moving people, changing their attitudes, and influencing their actions—that is, when it is brought into contact with their existing system of aims and purposes. When we think of knowledge as valuable in itself, we are always assuming something about the kind of understanding that underlies and connects the various pieces of information to form a coherent worldview.[15] That view cannot come from science in isolation because it involves a wider understanding of the life around the knower.

Thus, the great scientists who have done so much to shape our present way of thinking have done it by expressing such a comprehensive vision, one that they did not draw only from science. They knew that it was vital that they consider other sources in their culture, and they often discussed those sources readily. Galileo and T. H. Huxley, Einstein and Bohr, Schrödinger, Heisenberg, and Haldane all consciously and deliberately philosophised, skilfully using profound ideas drawn from those who had thought about these problems before them. None of these men would have accepted for a moment the idea of science as an isolated imperial power, at war with other intellectual disciplines and anxious only to subdue them.

How, then, do the scientistic writers we have been considering fit into this tradition? They are undoubtedly within it in so far as they, too, aim to promote a particular worldview rather than merely furnishing neutral facts. When all these writers use the word "science," they mean a particular kind of scientific spirit or attitude that includes far more than a mere set of facts or a curiosity about facts. Nehru saw this wider attitude not as neutral but as the bearer of new values, as a moral force that *alone* could solve all his problems. He personified it, speaking of "those who make friends with science" rather than just of those who use it. He saw it not as a mere tool but as a powerful ally in the battle against "superstition and deadening custom and tradition."

Supposing we were to ask Nehru, can he really rely on science *alone*? Isn't he also going to need good laws, effective administrators, honest and intelligent politicians, good new customs to replace the old ones, and perhaps even a sensitive understanding of the traditions that he means to sweep away? Might he not even need to know a good deal of history and anthropology before he starts on his destructive cleansing of tradition? Now, of course, Nehru knows he is going to need all these things. But he is assuming that they are all included in what he means by science. He includes in "science" the whole worldview that he takes to lie behind it, namely, the decent, humane, liberal attitude out of which it has (in fact) grown. In fact, he expects to buy the whole Enlightenment as part of the package. He has faith in the Enlightenment's philosophy as well as in its chemical discoveries. He expects that the scientific spirit will include within it wise and benevolent use of those discoveries. He is certainly not thinking of science as something likely to produce industrial pollution, or the invention of refined methods of torture, or opportunities for profiteering, or a concentration on weaponry, or overuse of chemicals on farms, or computer viruses, or irresponsible currency speculation made possible by the latest computers, or the wholesale waste of resources on gadgetry. The prophets of this scientistic movement expected from the thing they called "science" nothing less than a new and better ethics, a direct basis for morals, and a distinctive set of values which would replace the earlier ones supplied by religion. They hoped that it would simply supersede and replace all the corruption and confusion of traditional ethical thinking. They did not—and their successors still do not—notice that the ethical component of this package is something much wider and actually quite independent of the science. At first they identified their new scientific values quite simply (as Nehru did) with those that the Enlightenment had brought in as a reaction against Christianity, values that were already an accepted part of Western culture. But as time went on, they became bolder and really did try to produce something new. In these more confident moods, they thought—and their successors still think—of the new scientific values not as a contribution to an existing ethical culture, not as an outgrowth of it, not even as something harmonious with it, but as a conquering invader that must replace it.

That faith powered the huge exaltation of science which has gripped so many would-be reformers from the mid-nineteenth to the mid-twentieth century. It promised a new wisdom, a decisive spiritual and moral advance. Later disillusionment on this topic centres, I think, even more on the failure of this spiritual and moral project than on the mixed results of actual scientific practice. Certainly, new technologies have often done harm as well as good, but the harm has been largely due to the lack of the promised new wisdom.

We must surely wonder now why so many people expected this wisdom to appear. That expectation set up a kind of cargo cult which is only now giving way to blank disappointment. From Thomas Hobbes and Francis Bacon to Auguste Comte and B. F. Skinner, scientistic prophets have regularly made Nehru's mistake of expecting the wrong kind of thing from science. They have been unconscious flatterers who got it the wrong kind of reputation. They have built up a distorted notion of what science itself is. What they promoted as scientific thinking was actually a series of uncriticised ideologies that gradually diverged from mainstream Enlightenment thinking in various alarming directions. The first ideology that claimed to be specially scientific in this way was Marxism. But Marxism did at least appear explicitly as a thought system based on argument. It was accordingly open to philosophical attack. Its successors, however, tended to bypass this dangerous stage, claiming rather to be parts of science itself and to share its absolute authority. That is why, when disappointment followed, it was science itself that became discredited. And this disappointment was bound to follow, partly because the good things that these prophets offered could not be supplied, partly (as we shall see) because some of the things they offered were not good at all.

False Objectivity; Turning People into Things

So what was this new ideology? The most obvious point about it—its hostility to religion—is actually a superficial one. It is true that, from the eighteenth century on, scientistic prophets have tended to be anti-Christian, holding that Christianity had failed to purify society and ought somehow to be replaced by science. This project was eagerly attempted in the Russian Revolution, but the results were disappointing. State atheism has proved to be just as compatible with crime and folly as state religion, and it is not at all clear that atheism itself has anything particular to do with physical science. In any case, whatever the faults of religion, science cannot sensibly be put in its place.

The functions of science and religion within a society are simply too different for this idea of a competition between them to make much sense once one begins to consider it seriously. Rivalry between them looks plausible only when both elements are stated in very crude forms (as, of course, they often are) or when the power groups that run these two concerns conflict at the political level. Political entanglement with power groups has notoriously been corrupting to religion, and it is no less so for science. Tribal drumbeating for it tends to confirm the distorted idea of science as an ideology able to direct the whole of life. It reverses the excellent move that Galileo and his colleagues made when they narrowed the province of physics by excluding from it all questions about purpose and meaning.

Throughout the twentieth century, scientistic prophets have repeatedly told a bewildered public that policies which in fact had little to do with science must be accepted because experts had shown that they were scientific and objective. A central example of this is the behaviorist doctrine that psychology, in order to be scientific, must deal only with people's outward behavior, ignoring motives and emotions and regarding them not just as unknowable but as trivial and causally ineffectual. This has led to many bizarre practical policies, such as the advice which J. B. Watson and B. F. Skinner gave to parents, that they should not hug or kiss their children but should treat them in a detached and distant manner, "like young adults." This treatment (they said) was necessary because it was scientific and objective.[16]

What made this approach seem scientific was certainly not the fact that it rested on research showing the success of these child-rearing methods. (If there had been any such research, it would have produced the opposite result.) Instead, the behaviorists' attitude seems surely to have been itself an emotional one, expressing a suspicion that affectionate behavior was dangerously human, something beneath the dignity of scientists. It seems to have flowed from fear of the conflicts and complications that attend ordinary human feeling. In order to escape these problems, psychologists stereotyped feeling in general as something "soft," something that was the business of the humanities, not the sciences. The same kind of prejudice has also operated in medicine, especially in psychiatry, where a similar retreat from attending to the feelings of patients has also often been recommended as *objective* and *scientific*. In such cases, the mere fact of reversing a tradition and attacking ordinary feeling has often been enough to suggest that the claim was scientific, as Nehru's language shows.

Perhaps the most striking case of this distorted approach, however, is industrial Taylorism, which was commonly known quite simply as scientific management. This is the philosophy of the conveyor belt, the view that workers ought to be treated like any other physical component on the production line. Any reference to their own point of view was then seen as subjective and thus an illicit, unscientific distraction. Neither the economists who devised this approach nor Henry Ford, who accepted it, thought of it simply as a quick way of making money. They saw it as something much grander, as scientific progress, a laudable extension of physical science into realms formerly ruled by sentiment and superstition. It seemed obvious to them that it was "subjective" to pay any attention to subjectivity.

Another favored way of appearing scientific is, of course, simply to mention quantities rather than qualities. Thus, policies can be called scientific if they involve counting or measuring something, never mind whether that particular thing needs to be counted or not, and never mind what use is being made of the resulting data. Anybody who is using some statistics can make this claim. Reliance on the citation index, on exams, and on the league tables that compare exam results are examples of this habit. Similarly, the American spin doctor Dick Morris lately claimed scientific status, saying that all he does is to "reduce the mysterious ways of politics to scientific testing and evaluation."

It is also often seen as scientific to talk as if people were actually and literally machines. This machine imagery has been so useful in many scientific contexts that many people no longer think of it as a metaphor but as a scientific fact. Thus, much as they might say "soot is just carbon" or "penguins are just birds," they remark in passing that the human brain is just a computer made of meat. They don't think of it as a metaphor at all.

This machine imagery became entrenched at the dawn of modern science because in the seventeenth century scientists were fascinated, as well they might be, by the ingenious clockwork automata of the day. They naturally hoped to extend this clockwork model, which worked so well for the solar system, to cover the whole of knowledge, and as the Industrial Revolution went on, that hope seemed more and more natural. But physics, the original source of this dream, has now largely abandoned it. The machine model has proved unsuitable for many central purposes, along with the simple atomic theory that fitted it. Indeed, physics has dropped the whole idea that the basic structure of matter is bound to prove perfectly simple, an idea which seemed obvious to seventeenth-century thinkers and which made the abstractions of the machine model look so plausible. Today, even for inorganic matter and still more for organisms, complexity is the name of the game.

Rationality Is Not an Algorithm

Perhaps I need not go over any more of these cases in which words like *scientific, objective,* and *machine* are used with this kind of biased sense. We meet them all the time. I want, however, to say plainly what should surely be obvious, namely that, in exposing these rhetorical attempts to turn science into a comprehensive ideology, I am not attacking science but defending it against a dangerous misconstruction.

These doctrines are not part of science. They are burgeoning fungi that have grown on it and done it a great deal of harm. It is no wonder at all that they produce "antiscience" feeling. People who fear science are chiefly disturbed by these imperialistic ideologies that import irrelevant, inhuman standards into nonscientific aspects of life and lead people to neglect the relevant ones. Throughout the social sciences and often in the humanities too, distorted ideas of what it means to be scientific and objective still direct a great deal of life and a great deal of research. The crude dualism that treats mind and body as separate, disconnected things still leads people to take sides between them and to suppose that, having opted for body, they have to get rid of mind by ignoring subjectivity. The trouble lies in the exclusivity, the either/or approach, the conviction that only one very simple way of thought is rational.

Even within science itself, this simplistic approach is beginning to make trouble. Our familiar stereotype of scientific rationality is still modelled on the methods of seventeenth-century physics. As I have mentioned, for many purposes modern physics has moved away from those methods. But not everybody in biology has heard the news of this change. Many biologists still tend to see mechanism as the only truly scientific thought pattern because they still think it is central to physics. And for some time, this belief has concentrated their attention strongly on microbiological questions, leading them to neglect larger-scale matters such as the behavior of whole organisms. Now, however, a number of biologists are suggesting that this neglect is gravely unbalancing biology.[17] (It certainly seems odd to think how much trouble Darwin might have had if he had applied today to get a research grant for his project, since it concentrated entirely on the behavior of whole organisms and on species.) Efforts are therefore being made to bring these larger units into focus again, thus "putting the life back into biology," as Lynn Margulis and Dorion Sagan put it.[18] Even the largest unit of all—Gaia, the biosphere within which we all live—is no longer outlawed as unscientific but is beginning to serve as a useful focus of ecological enquiry.

In psychology (to end this rather crude lightning tour) the taboo that the behaviorists imposed on the study of consciousness has lately been lifted. That astonishing Berlin Wall has finally come down. Consciousness is at last admitted to be significant and is being studied, with results that are confusing but will surely be fertile.[19] So this is one more area where narrow, distorted rulings on *what it is to be scientific* are crumbling fast.

Wild Hopes

As I said earlier, the trouble with Enlightenment myths when they get out of hand is that they tend to exalt the form over the substance of what is being said, the method over the aim of an activity, and precision of detail over completeness of cover. In all the areas of science just mentioned, the pseudo-scientific ideology that we have been considering has done this. In all of them, it is now being questioned, and we surely need to intensify this process.

We need to stop treating "science" as a single monolithic entity, a solid kingdom embattled against rival kingdoms. On the one hand, the various sciences differ. Ecology and anthropology are not at all like physics, nor indeed is biology, and this is not disastrous because they don't have to be like it. And, on the other hand, we need to stop treating this entity called "science" as an expanding empire, destined one day to take over the rest of the intellectual world. Our current problems about the environment and about human rights are large problems which need cooperative work from every kind of intellectual discipline, from ethics to computing, from anthropology to law, and from Russian history to soil science. The intense academic specialisation that prevails today makes this cooperation hard enough already without adding the extra obstacles imposed by tribal warfare. Scientistic imperialism has been closely connected with the attempt to reduce all the various sciences to a single model, as is clear from the way in which the unity of science movement in the United States has devoted itself to asserting omnicompetence. Both errors, in fact, spring equally from an unduly narrow, monopolistic concept of rationality, a concept which we still draw essentially from seventeenth-century philosophers and above all from Descartes. (This is just one more case in which people who refuse to have anything to do with philosophy have become enslaved to outdated forms of it.)

When Descartes started on his famous quest for absolute certainty, he did not, as his writings suggest, set out with a quite open mind about where he might find it. He already had his eye on Galileo. Already, he had decided that the kind of logical clarity found in this new mathematical physics could make it infallible. He therefore thought it the only light that the human intellect could safely follow. This meant that the methods of that science must somehow be extended to cover all other subject matters as well as physics. Eventually, mathematical physics would unite the whole of knowledge in a Theory of Everything, a unified rational system balanced securely on a single foundation.

Thus, the Enlightenment notion of physical science was imperialistic from the outset. From its birth, the idea of this science was associated with two strangely ambitious claims, infallibility and the power of imposing one order on the whole of thought. We know now that these two soaring ambitions can't be achieved and that they don't need to. Rationality does not require that we should be infallible, nor that we should have all our knowledge tightly organised on the model of mathematics. But we are still haunted by the idea that these things are necessary.

In spite of his own interest in consciousness, Descartes put physics in a position where it was more or less forced to claim an intellectual monopoly over the whole of knowledge. This arrangement demanded a kind of materialism that, in the end, was bound to leave mind with no apparent standing room in the universe. Later philosophers saw this clearly enough. But most of them were just as convinced as he was that they needed a comprehensive, unified system. So, instead of trying to bridge the strange gap he had placed between mind and matter, idealists and materialists responded by fighting prolonged wars to decide which of these two superpowers should control the whole system.

That conflict is still with us today. On the one side, idealism, though it is not now much mentioned, still functions as a shadowy background to many sceptical "postmodern" doctrines such as extreme constructivism. On the other, dogmatic materialists still see this metaphysical feud as a living issue, a battle that must be won. Surely we need to step back and ask what the disagreement is actually about. The really surprising thing about both contestants is what they have in common. They are both still convinced that such a comprehensive thought system is necessary and possible. They do not think we can be rational without it.

Objectivity Has Degrees

Our next question is, how would we manage without such a system? How does science (or how do the many sciences) relate to the rest of our thought? How can we bring subjectivity and objectivity together in our thinking? What should we substitute for the current pattern that shows matter, described by a single objective system called science, on one side of the gap confronting a mass of indescribable subjective experience on the other?

Here we need to see what a strange myth the notion of a gap always was. In reality, our experience is not sharply divided into mind and matter, into subjective and objective points of view. It spreads across a continuous plain. Virtually all our thought integrates material taken from both the objective and the subjective angles. And we have, by now, formed very useful concepts for doing this. Thus, dentists are not baffled when they have to bring together the objective facts that make up their professional knowledge with the subjective report that patients give of their various pains. Indeed, dentists may in turn be patients themselves. When these dentists think or talk about their own toothache, they can use a whole familiar tool kit of conceptual schemes which connect the inside with the outside position intelligibly.

Objectivity, in fact, is not just a single standpoint. It is one of two directions in which thought can move. As Thomas Nagel puts it, when we want to acquire a more objective understanding of some aspect of life in the world,

> we step back from our initial view of it and form a new conception which has that view and its relation to the world as its object. . . . The process can be repeated, yielding a still more objective conception. . . . The distinction between

more subjective and more objective views is really a matter of degree.... *The standpoint of morality is more objective than that of private life, but less objective than the standpoint of physics.*[20] (my emphasis)

Thus, we compare elements derived from two or more angles in various ways that suit the different matters we are discussing, ways that differ widely according to the purpose of our thought at the time—perhaps much as we combine the very different data from sight and touch in our sense perception. As Nagel points out, increased objectivity is not always a virtue, nor is it always useful for explanation. A dentist who decides to become more objective by ignoring the pain of his patients will not thereby become a better dentist.

How, then, do we actually manage to relate these various ways of thinking and their various degrees of objectivity when we use them together in our lives? The fashionable reductive pattern tells us that, in order to connect different families of concepts, we should arrange them in a linear sequence running from the superficial to the fundamental and ending with the most fundamental group of all—namely, physics.[21] That hierarchy fills the whole space available for explanation. The more fundamental thought patterns are then called "hard" and the upper ones "soft." This rather mysterious tactile metaphor means that the upper or softer layers are only provisional. They are more superficial, amateurish, or nonserious because they fall short of the ultimate explanation. Classed as folk psychology, these layers must only be tolerated as makeshifts to be used until the real scientific account is available or when it is too cumbersome for convenience. They are just stages on the way down to the only fully mature science, which is physics.

The metaphor of *levels*, which is often used to describe the relation between these various ways of thinking, seems to endorse this linear pattern. But it really is not clear what sense this idea of a one-dimensional hierarchy could ever make. It can only work if the relation between physics and chemistry (which is its original model) can be repeated again and again, not only for biology but beyond it to colonise other branches of thought such as history, logic, law, linguistics, ethics, musicology, and mathematics, and to translate them all eventually into physical terms. Nobody has ever tried to do this, and it is not easy to see how they could even start. (History alone is an impossible case, and since historical method is needed in science itself—for instance, in cosmology and in the study of evolution—that failure should finish the matter.) Indeed, the project remains so desperately vague that I suggest we should put this whole linear pattern aside for the moment and consider a quite different conceptual map, one drawn from the homeland of all maps, geography.

The Many-Maps Model

In our atlases, we find a great many maps of the world. Mine offers world physiography, world climatology, world vegetation, world political, world food, world airlines, and a great many more. They all represent the world differently. But there are not many worlds. How do we relate these varying pictures?

We do not need to pick on one of these maps as fundamental. We do not need to find a single atomic structure belonging to that map and justify the other patterns by reducing them to it. Finally, we do not need to bring in physics, which has already done that atomising job for us. What we need is something different. We have to relate all these patterns in a way that shows the relation between them, that shows why there is room for them all and why they are not rival pictures showing separate alternative worlds.

As John Ziman pointed out, we are called on to perform this same feat in a still more striking way whenever we relate the Underground map of a city such as London to the much more complicated street map. We are not forced, then, to conclude that the Underground map is more fundamental because it is simpler, any more than we are forced to respect it more because it shows us a deeper level of the city.[22] And we make connections of the same kind whenever we relate what one special way of thinking—say, poetry or anthropology or history or medicine—tells us about the human heart.

In order to make these connections, we always draw back to look at the larger context of thought within which the questions arise that lead to these various ways of thinking. Explanation, in fact, works by widening the context, not by atomising the structure. There is nothing irrational about this outward move. We know that the different maps are meant to answer different sorts of questions, questions that arise from different angles. All these questions concern the same enormous world, which can rightly be described in all these ways because it is bigger than all of them.[23] Rationality itself demands this pluralistic approach because it is the only way to do justice to the complexity of the facts we encounter in experience. This complexity is no threat to reason. Nor is the fact that our set of maps is never exhaustive. Reason does not ask us to pretend that we can answer all questions about the world or that we could ever do so. It would surely be highly irrational for evolved terrestrial creatures like ourselves to claim this power.[24] Today, we can readily admit that there is logical space left around and between our maps because we ourselves are a definite, limited kind of being. We do not need to claim, as seventeenth-century theorists did, the power to provide a supermap uniting all the maps in a single comprehensive system.

If, then, we ask how we actually do relate our various maps, the simple answer is that we do it by following the coastlines that appear on all of them showing common patterns which refer us back to the larger context. For instance, political maps, especially maps of Africa and Australia, often show mysterious straight lines not found in most other maps. (There are no straight lines in nature.) The only way to understand these straight lines is to relate them to the history of particular treaties and, beyond that, to the colonial system that produced them. Treaties, however, are not things that can be explained in terms of physiography or vegetation or electrons. Nor can they be explained in terms of the neurons of the people who make them, any more than the people themselves can. The only way to explain treaties is by thinking about human history and human purposes. And this is talk that cuts into the cosmic cake (so to speak) from a quite different angle.

Understanding the relation of history to physiography is not, then, like relating two places on the same map. It involves relating two maps—two distinct ways of thinking—to one another. And when we consider problems about how the physical sciences relate to our conscious experience and more generally to the rest of life, that is what we have to do. This work is philosophical, but that does not mean that it has to be left to philosophers. Like the further understanding of problems about human rights, it is a cooperative venture, one to which all citizens of the intellectual republic can contribute. And for all these citizens, it is a much more interesting and useful occupation than the wars recommended by competitive imperialism.

Notes

1. C. H. Waddington, *The Scientific Attitude* (Harmondsworth: Penguin, 1941), p. 170.

2. René Descartes, *Discourse on Method*, pt. two.

3. For a drastic questioning of this claim, see Ken Booth, "Human Wrongs and International Relations," *International Affairs* 71 (1995), pp. 103–126.

4. I have discussed this point more fully in my book *Heart and Mind* (London: Methuen, 1983).

5. See Garret Hardin, "Living on a Lifeboat," *Bioscience* (October 1974), and more fully in *The Limits of Altruism* (Bloomington: Indiana University Press, 1977). I am not sure who produced the rival image, but Hardin's whole argument was well discussed by Peter Singer in his *Practical Ethics* (Cambridge: Cambridge University Press, 1979), where further reading may be found on this whole debate.

6. For further discussion of this useful concept, see Timothy Dunne and Nicholas Wheeler, eds., *Human Rights in Global Politics* (forthcoming, Cambridge: Cambridge University Press, 1998).

7. I have discussed the kind of relativism that would make this agreement seem impossible in *Can't We Make Moral Judgements?* (Bristol: The Bristol Press,

1991) and, more briefly, in "On Trying Out One's New Sword," chap. 5 in *Heart and Mind*.

8. See Edward Wilson's book *Biophilia: The Human Bond with Other Species* (Cambridge, Mass.: Harvard University Press, 1984).

9. See James Lovelock, *Gaia: The Practical Science of Planetary Medicine* (London: Gaia Books Limited, 1991).

10. I have discussed this twofold difficulty about the word "postmodern" in my introduction to the revised paperback edition of *Beast and Man* (London: Routledge, 1995), p. xxvii.

11. *Tomorrow's World* was, for many years, the most popular and informative science programme on British television.—*Ed.*

12. Rudolf Carnap, *The Logical Structure of the World*, trans. R. George (Berkeley: University of California Press, 1967), p. 290. For a fuller discussion of such claims, see the first chapter of Tom Sorell, *Scientism: Philosophy and the Infatuation with Science* (London: Routledge, 1994).

13. See Peter Atkins's article, "The Limitless Power of Science," in John Cornwell, ed., *Nature's Imagination: The Frontiers of Scientific Vision* (Oxford: Oxford University Press, 1995), pp. 122–133.

14. Pandit Nehru, quoted in *Proceedings of the National Institute of Science of India* 27 (1960), p. 564.

15. I have discussed these issues more fully in *Wisdom, Information and Wonder: What Is Knowledge For?* (London: Routledge, 1989).

16. See John B. Watson, *Psychological Care of Infant and Child* (New York: W. W. Norton, 1928), pp. 5–6, 9–10, and 82–83, and a good discussion of such passages by Barbara Ehrenreich and Deirdre English in *For Her Own Good: 150 Years of the Experts' Advice to Women* (London: Pluto Press, 1979), pp. 183–185. On Skinner, see the child-rearing arrangements in his early utopia, *Walden Two*.

17. See two excellent recent books: Brian Goodwin, *How the Leopard Changed Its Spots* (London: Weidenfeld and Nicolson, 1994), and Steven Rose, *Lifelines: Biology, Freedom and Determinism* (London: Allen Lane, Penguin Press, 1997).

18. In Lynn Margulis and Dorion Sagan, *What Is Life?* (London: Weidenfeld and Nicolson, 1995), p. 1.

19. This process may now be watched in the lively pages of the *Journal of Consciousness Studies*, which was born in 1994.

20. Thomas Nagel, *The View from Nowhere* (Oxford: Oxford University Press, 1986), p. 5.

21. A clear, typically confident statement of this orthodox view may be found in E. O. Wilson, *On Human Nature* (Cambridge, Mass.: Harvard University Press, 1978), pp. 7–10.

22. John Ziman, *Reliable Knowledge* (Cambridge: Cambridge University Press, 1978), pp. 82–85.

23. I have developed this point more fully in "One World—But a Big One," *Journal of Consciousness Studies* 3, nos. 5–6 (1996).

24. Daniel Dennett, however, does make this astonishing claim in *Darwin's Dangerous Idea* (Harmondsworth: Penguin, 1996), pp. 381–383, opposing Noam Chomsky's and Colin McGinn's reasonable suggestion that our faculties are subject at some point to "cognitive closure." Dennett relies largely there on assuming that the burden of proof must fall on his opponents, something that is scarcely obvious.

About the Editor
and Contributors

John D. Barrow is director of the Astronomy Centre at the University of Sussex. He has taught at Oxford and Berkeley and is the author of nine books exploring the broader ramifications of developments in astronomy, physics, and mathematics. These include *The Left Hand of Creation, The Anthropic Cosmic Principle, Pi in the Sky,* and *The Artful Universe.* He lectures around the world and has the curious distinction of having lectured at 10 Downing St, Windsor Castle, and the Vatican Palace.

Richard Dawkins is professor of the public understanding of science at Oxford University and professorial fellow of New College, Oxford. Born in Africa and educated at Oxford, he taught at the University of California at Berkeley before returning to a readership in zoology at Oxford. He is the author of the bestselling books *The Selfish Gene, The Blind Watchmaker, The Extended Phenotype, River out of Eden,* and *Climbing Mount Improbable.*

Daniel C. Dennett is distinguished arts and sciences professor, professor of philosophy, and director of the Centre for Cognitive Studies at Tufts University. He studied philosophy at Harvard and Oxford and has been visiting professor at universities throughout the world. He is codirector of the Curricular Software Studio at Tufts and has designed numerous museum exhibits on computers. He has written widely on various aspects of the mind, and his books include *Content and Consciousness, Brainstorms, Elbow Room, Consciousness Explained, Darwin's Dangerous Idea,* and *Kinds of Minds.*

Nicholas Humphrey is professor of Psychology at the New School for Social Research, New York. Educated at Cambridge, he discovered "blindsight," first in monkeys, and later he confirmed its existence in humans. Continuing work with the sensory preferences of animals developed his interest in the psychology of aesthetics and human cognitive capacities. His publications include *Consciousness Regained: Chapters in the Development of the Mind, A History of the Mind, Soul Searching,* and the successful television series *The Inner Eye.*

Mary Midgley was formerly senior lecturer in philosophy at the University of Newcastle upon Tyne. A moral philosopher, she has taken a particular interest in humankind's relation to the other species in the process of evolution. She has also written extensively on scientific doctrine as a religious rhetoric. Her books include *Beast and Man; Animals and Why They Matter; Wickedness; Science as Salvation;* and *Utopias, Dolphins and Computers.*

George Monbiot is founder of *The Land Is Ours* campaign. Involved in direct-action campaigns throughout Britain, he was the 1995 winner of the UN Global

Award for Outstanding Environmental Achievement. As a result of his campaigns, he is persona non grata in seven countries and has a life sentence in absentia in Indonesia. He is the author of *Poisoned Arrows, Amazon Watershed,* and *No Man's Land,* all of which were accompanied by series on public radio. He also writes a column for the *Guardian.*

Jonathan Rée is professor of philosophy at Middlesex University and director of the Centre for Research in Modern European Philosophy. He has taken a particular interest in the history of the social and rhetorical dimensions of continental philosophical writing. His books include studies of Kierkegaard, Sartre, and Descartes; *Philosophical Tales;* and *Philosophy and Its Past.*

Wes Williams is a fellow and tutor in French at New College, Oxford. He has co-written a number of plays and screenplays and is the author of *The Undiscovered Country: Pilgrimage and Narrative in the French Renaissance* (Oxford: Oxford University Press, 1998).